UNQUENCHABLE

JOY

21 Weeks to Discovering God's Overcoming Power

Bible
Study

Kimberly Tyler

ISBN: 978-1-966798-34-7

This book is dedicated to my incredible sister Kathleen,

You've taught me that joy isn't about having a perfect life but having a heart that trusts in a perfect Savior. You've shown me what it means to smile through storms, to laugh even when the world says you shouldn't, and to find beauty in the everyday miracles we often overlook.

Your faith has been a steady example for many, your hope, a reflection of God's love, and your perseverance, a reminder that joy can coexist with struggle.

This study on joy is inspired by you—a woman who understands that joy is both a gift and a choice, a wellspring we return to in good times and lean on when life feels heavy.

Thank you for showing me what it looks like to live with joy, grace, and faith. I pray this book blesses others the way you have blessed me.

With all my heart,
your loving sister, Kimberly

Table of Contents

Introduction..7

Chapter One: Unquenchable Joy-Week 1...9

Chapter Two: Unquenchable Joy-Week 2.. 13

Chapter Three: Unquenchable Joy-Week 3 18

Chapter Four: Unquenchable Joy-Week 4 24

Chapter Five: Unquenchable Joy-Week 5 29

Chapter Six: Unquenchable Joy-Week 6 34

Chapter Seven: Unquenchable Joy-Week 7...39

Chapter Eight: Unquenchable Joy-Week 8 45

Chapter Nine: Unquenchable Joy-Week 9 50

Chapter Ten: Unquenchable Joy-Week 10....................................... 56

Chapter Eleven: Unquenchable Joy-Week 11 62

Chapter Twelve: Unquenchable Joy-Week 12 68

Chapter Thirteen: Unquenchable Joy-Week 13 73

Chapter Fourteen: Unquenchable Joy-Week 14 79

Chapter Fifteen: Unquenchable Joy-Week 15 83

Chapter Sixteen: Unquenchable Joy-Week 16 88

Chapter Seventeen: Unquenchable Joy-Week 17.............................94

Chapter Eighteen: Unquenchable Joy-Week 18......................... 100

Chapter Nineteen: Unquenchable Joy-Week 19 105

Chapter Twenty: Unquenchable Joy-Week 20 110

Chapter Twenty-One: Unquenchable Joy-Week 21..........................115

Scripture Resources 122

About the Author.. 127

Introduction

In today's busy world, most of us struggle to find a few moments of quiet time to devote to our growth in the Word. I have dedicated this Bible study to my sister. In many ways, she is my hero, and I look up to her for her personal accomplishments and the way she has clung to the Lord despite the many crashing waves that have sought to separate her from Him. She has often told me that many of the books she has read have been difficult for her to stick with due to the vocabulary used by the author and/or the complexity of the text and material.

This study is not designed to be a deep theological study. Instead, I have purposely tried to keep the Bible study format simple and accessible. I hold several degrees and credentials, but I have never attended seminary and do not hold a theology degree. This Bible study on the topic of Joy is simply designed to encourage time in the Word with 21 weekly studies, questions to promote reflection, suggestions, and encouragement on the practical application of the study to the reader's lives, and ends with a simple prayer.

The weekly study is also a weekly meditation as it is short and can be re-read and reviewed throughout the week for a deeper understanding. I have also provided additional resources in the appendix if a reader desires more study. You cannot have too much soaking in the Word as it provides an opportunity for the Holy Spirit to speak to you and reveal Himself to you.

I encourage you to find a church with a mature and knowledgeable pastor and attend regularly for maximum growth in your spiritual life. I am extremely fortunate to have a pastor who is very studied in the Word and can take very complex concepts and make them easy to understand and apply to your life, something I truly appreciate.

Each week's study and meditation contains 3–7 verses. Together, the words joy and rejoice appear over 300 times in the King James Version of the Bible. When you add in all the other forms of the word, such as joyful and rejoicing, the usage grows to over 500 times in many versions of the Bible. Out of all the books in the Bible, it is used the most in Philippians, where the apostle Paul uses it 16 times in only 104 verses, earning Philippians the title of "The Epistle of Joy." Written while Paul was imprisoned, the major theme is rejoicing in every circumstance.

This study only uses a fraction or a small amount of the verses on Joy in the Bible, but the reader is encouraged to find and read all of them if desired. The reader is also encouraged to pick one of the verses used in the weekly study and meditation and work to memorize it. Write it on a card you carry with you, put it in your notes on your phone, or put it on a Post-it note on a mirror in the bathroom where you brush your teeth. Strategies for memorization include memorizing 3–4 words at a time, then stringing them together, or using the old-fashioned way of writing the verse several times. These are all very effective memorization methods. Hiding God's Word in our hearts is always beneficial to us, especially in times of trouble when the Holy Spirit can bring it to our remembrance.

This simple study is designed to be used individually or with a group of friends. Read the study/meditation by yourself, write the answers to the reflection and application sections, and then pray the simple prayer of thanksgiving for the new and deeper revelation you have received. Each week, take a few moments to review the prior week's study and reflect on the application that week. Find encouragement in any progress you make, and remember, two steps forward and one step back is still progress for those challenging weeks where you may need to revisit your application steps. Most of all, rejoice always in the Lord and encourage others to rejoice in the Lord!

Chapter One

Unquenchable Joy-Week 1

"Though you have not seen Him, you love Him. Though
you do not now see Him, you believe in Him and rejoice
with joy that is inexpressible and filled with glory."
1 Peter 1:8

Study and Meditation for the Week: Relationship

Life's daily and long-term goals and visions can be compelling and uplifting, full of hope and promise, leading us to plan and expand our horizons and dreams. I love to set visions, plan for tomorrow, and make audacious or very bold goals; the bigger, the better. It energizes me and gives me a sense of joyful purpose. I also identify with people who dream big and love to hear of their accomplishments and victories. But I can also experience a sense of failure and disappointment when I fall short of my own goals or the ones the world has set for me. I have come to realize that I am not alone in that, as I have seen women share the same challenges and difficulties.

It's easy to see that for many women, in navigating the complexities of modern life and all its pressures, the pursuit of joy can often feel elusive or hard to find, and when we do manage to find it, it is fleeting or short-lived. However, the Bible presents a profound truth, that actual, lasting joy is not a fleeting emotion but an unquenchable, unshakeable force that provides lasting energy, enthusiasm, and peace and can be a strong foundation for enduring happiness. By embracing biblical principles and wholeheartedly following Jesus Christ's commandments, it is possible to cultivate a joy-filled life that abides or remains and even thrives in the face of adversity or conditions that are against us and try to take us down.

As a friend and sister, let me share the secret to unquenchable joy: a deep, personal relationship with Jesus Christ. This relationship is not just a distant acquaintance but an intimate connection that transforms our hearts and minds. Jesus Himself invites us into this relationship, promising abundant, lasting joy. In **John 15:11**, He says, **"I have told you this so that My joy may be in you and that your joy may be complete."**

This joy is not dependent on external circumstances but flows from knowing and being known by the Creator of the universe. When we draw near to Jesus, we experience His presence, which fills us with an indescribable and glorious joy (see our opening scripture, **1 Peter 1:8**).

This unquenchable joy then becomes our strength, as **Nehemiah 8:10** declares, **"The joy of the Lord is your strength."** and **Isaiah 59:19** says, **"When the enemy comes in like a flood, the Lord shall lift up a standard against him."**

Jesus' joy is not like the fleeting happiness the world gives. It is deep, abiding, and unquenchable, not even a flood of trouble can stop or stand against it. It sustains us through life's highs and lows, energizing us with enthusiasm and hope. The joy of the Lord is a powerful force that can transform our lives, making us strong, resilient, able to rebound fully, and capable of facing any challenge with a positive outlook and overcoming it as victorious champions.

As we align our lives with biblical principles, we begin to be established in this joy that is unquenchable even in the floods that may come upon us in life and will see ourselves rooted in that joy more deeply each day. As we come to see that these principles are not burdensome rules but life-giving truths that guide us into God's perfect will, we will be able to embrace them even more fully and apply them to our lives, which will give us a firm foundation for living a truly joyful life that is not based on our circumstances or life's challenges.

Psalm 19:8 affirms, **"The precepts of the Lord are right, giving joy to the heart."** By living according to God's Word, we position ourselves to receive His blessings and experience His energizing and joy. The scriptures reveal several simple but foundational daily practices we can focus on to help cultivate and apply these truths to our lives. We will look at these truth principles in the coming weeks.

Reflection and Discussion Questions:

As we meditate on this week's study verses: **1 Peter 1:8, John 15:11, Nehemiah 8:10, Isaiah 59:19, and Psalm 19:8, what common theme** is the Lord showing or revealing to you about joy?

_____

_____

What do you think the Lord Jesus **would like you to understand from these verses** about His joy and how it completely fills, strengthens, and transforms the lives of those who love and obey Him?

_____

_____

Application:

What are **two (2) practical ways** we can apply what we have studied to our lives this coming week?

1._____

_____

2._____

_____

What good things do you expect to happen as we apply these truths to our lives?

1._____

_____

2._____

_____

Simple Prayer:

Lord, thank you for loving us. Show us the fullness of Your joy as we walk by Your side, hand in hand, through our journey through this life. In Jesus' name, we pray. Amen.

Chapter Two

Unquenchable Joy-Week 2

"The Lord has done great things for us, and we are filled with joy." **Psalm 126:3**

Study and Meditation for the Week: Gratitude

A joyful heart naturally overflows with gratitude, especially when we step into God's presence, and a grateful heart is a joyful heart. This connection between joy and thankfulness is woven throughout scripture, showing us how tuning into God's blessings transforms how we feel and think. Cultivating a heart of gratitude isn't just a good idea; it's a powerful principle that can bring unshakable joy into our lives. And it's not hard—when we recognize the goodness God surrounds us with every day, joy and gratitude seem to come alive naturally in our hearts.

Paul explains this in **1 Thessalonians 5:16-18,** where he says, **"Rejoice always, pray continually, give thanks in all circumstances; for this is God's will for you in Christ Jesus."** We're told to rejoice, pray, and give thanks in all things because it aligns us with God's will. But how can we live this way every day? It's about shifting our focus and making small, intentional choices to recognize and thank God for what He's doing and has already done. Gratitude helps us see the blessings right in front of us and not just the things we're wishing for. And a simple habit of giving thanks can change our perspective in powerful ways.

Ezra 3:11 says, **"With praise and thanksgiving they sang to the Lord: 'He is good; his love toward Israel endures forever.'"** This was when the Israelites were finally rebuilding the temple after years of struggle and setbacks. They could've easily been frustrated, thinking about everything that went wrong in the past. But instead, they chose to sing with gratitude and joy, focusing on God's goodness rather than their challenges. This choice to rejoice wasn't because everything was perfect but because they believed in God's enduring love and faithfulness.

1 Chronicles 16:34 echoes this beautifully: **"Give thanks to the Lord, for he is good; his love endures forever."** Gratitude shifts our attention to God's unwavering love and strength even in the midst of our struggles. It's about seeing His presence in every situation and being thankful that He's always with us, steady and faithful.

The psalmist in **Psalm 126:3** says, **"The Lord has done great things for us, and we are filled with joy."** Reflecting on what God has done can fill our hearts with gratitude and joy, even when facing tough times. It's applying the principle we discussed last week of remembering that He's been faithful before and will continue to be in the future.

Let's look at a few practical ways we can cultivate a heart of gratitude in our lives.

1. **Start Each Day with Thanks:** Begin your day by listing three things you're grateful for. They don't have to be big—sometimes, the simplest things can remind us of God's goodness. By starting the day with this small exercise, we set a tone of gratitude and joy.

2. **Create a Gratitude Journal:** Keep a notebook or even a note on your phone where you jot down things that went well or moments you felt God's presence throughout the day. Over time, you'll build a record of God's goodness, and this will become your personal faith testimony to look back on during challenging times to remind you of His faithfulness to you.

3. **Speak It Out Loud:** Take a few minutes to say, "Thank you, God," for specific things throughout your day. Whether it's for a good conversation, a meal, or a beautiful moment in nature, voicing gratitude out loud helps cement joy in our hearts and reminds us that God's blessings are everywhere.

4. **Shift Your Perspective in Hard Times:** When challenges come, practice saying, "God, thank you for being with me through this." It's not easy, but acknowledging His presence even when things are tough can give us the strength to see hope and joy beyond the difficulty.

5. **Share Gratitude with Others:** It's contagious when we talk about the things we're grateful for! We inspire others to see the good in their own lives, and together, we cultivate an environment of joy and positivity.

Gratitude isn't just about finding the silver lining; it's about trusting God's goodness, whether times are easy or hard. When we take even a few moments to be grateful each day, it reshapes how we see life. We can stand firm, knowing we're held in God's love, and that brings us joy and peace. These simple practices make room for a heart full of joy that transcends circumstances and connects us to the goodness of God. So, let's keep looking for His blessings, big and small, and let joy and gratitude lead the way.

Reflection and Discussion Questions:

As we meditate on this week's study verses, **Psalm 126:3, 1 Thessalonians 5:16-18, Ezra 3:11, 1 Chronicles 16:34, and Psalm 126:3, what common theme** is the Lord showing or revealing to you about joy?

_____

_____

What do you think the Lord Jesus **would like you to understand from these verses** about His joy and how it fills, strengthens, and transforms the lives of those who love and obey Him?

_____

_____

Application:

What are **two (2) practical ways** we can apply what we have studied to our lives this coming week? You can choose from the list we discussed or create some of your own to try.

1._____

_____

2._____

_____

What good things do you expect to happen as we apply these truths to our lives?

1._____

_____

2._____

_____

Simple Prayer:

Father, I am grateful for you, your presence, your guidance, and your covering. Help me to always turn to you in times of need and express my appreciation for all the joy you provide. In Jesus' name, we pray. Amen.

Chapter Three

Unquenchable Joy-Week 3

*"Though you have not seen Him, you love Him; and
even though you do not see him now, you believe in Him
and are filled with an inexpressible and glorious joy."*
1 Peter 1:8

Study and Meditation for the Week: Faith

Faith is the bedrock of unquenchable joy. It is the unshakeable, solid foundation of our relationship with God. **Hebrews 11:1** defines Faith as **"Confidence in what we hope for and assurance about what we do not see."** Merriam-Webster defines it as a strong belief in something for which there is no proof. This firm confidence allows us to trust in God's promises and find joy in His faithfulness, even when we cannot yet see the total outcome. Faith allows us to trust that God's Word is true and His promises are sure with a solid belief. When we have strongly-rooted Faith that God is always with us and His presence is always near us, it brings us deep and abiding joy.

Psalm 16:11 reminds us, **"You make known to me the path of life; you will fill me with joy in your presence, with eternal pleasures at your right hand."** No matter where we are in our journey or what we may face, we can find joy in knowing God is an ever-present help, His Spirit abides in us, and His eyes are always on us.

Another important aspect or part of Faith is believing that God has a unique plan for every one of our lives and that those plans are very good. **Jeremiah 29:11** promises, **"For I know the plans I have for you,"** declares the Lord, **"plans to prosper you and not to harm you, plans to give you hope and a future."** When we have Faith that God's perfect plan for us is unfolding as it should in our lives, we find increased joy in His divine purpose for us. This is very important as we move forward in our journey.

We will have days when the plan doesn't look like it is working. We may experience unexpected setbacks that sometimes may feel overwhelming. That's when we have to look at the foundation of our Faith, the Solid Rock that is our Lord Jesus Christ. Remembering all that God has brought you through is also very helpful. We sometimes forget to acknowledge God's past faithfulness to us. In the Bible, people would build special altars and places of remembrance where they had gone through significant times and events with God. These markers were set in places where God had shown His faithfulness and love to them, so they would never forget it. Remembering our journey and the places He has brought us through helps us to grow in our Faith.

Paul connects the progress of growing in Faith with an increase in joy, indicating that joy deepens as our Faith grows. **Philippians 1:25—"Convinced of this, I know that I will remain, and I will continue with all of you for your progress and joy in the faith."** As we grow in our Faith as children of God, we learn to run to our Father more and more for genuine assurance and fullness of joy. The first thing a child wants to hear when they fall down or experience any crisis is the reassurance that it will be OK. As His children, we also have assurance through Faith that helps us stand up, wipe ourselves off, and keep going with Joy because we know we are standing by Faith on the invincible, unconquerable, undefeatable, unsurmountable truth of His word and who He is.

1 Peter 1:8-9 states, **"Though you have not seen him, you love him; and even though you do not see him now, you believe in him and are filled with an inexpressible and glorious joy, for you are receiving the end result of your faith, the salvation of your souls."**

As we meditate on these verses this week, may we discover more fully each day that Faith in Christ is the foundation of unquenchable joy, empowering us to trust in God's promises and love for us; here are a few simple, doable steps that can help you build a faith that's steady and strong, no matter what comes your way.

1. **Start Small with Time in the Word:** You don't need to read a whole chapter at once. Pick one verse, like **Hebrews 11:1** or **Jeremiah 29:11**, and sit with it. Let the words soak in. Ask God to show you what He wants you to understand. Over time, this simple habit will deepen your faith as His truth becomes a part of you.

2. **Make Prayer Your First Response:** When something happens—good, bad, or unexpected—talk to God about it right then. Whisper a "thank you" when you see a blessing or a quick "help me" when you're overwhelmed. Prayer builds trust, and trust builds faith. Remember **Psalm 62:8: "Pour out your hearts to Him, for God is our refuge."**

3. **Remember His Faithfulness:** Take a moment to think back on times when God came through for you. Write those moments down. God's faithfulness in the past reminds you that He's still working today and reinforces our joy. Just like the

altars in the Bible, as we practice building "remembrance altars" by recalling the Lord's past faithfulness and unwavering love, we allow Him to strengthen our Faith, confidence, and joy in Him.

4. **Surround Yourself with Faith Builders:** Play worship music that points your heart to God. Songs about His promises or His love can anchor your faith throughout the day. You can also listen to sermons, podcasts, or audio devotionals while driving or working. Let these messages remind you of who God is, what He's done in the past, and what He desires to do in your life.

5. **Take Steps of Trust:** Faith grows when you act on it. Is there something you've been hesitant to trust God with? Maybe it's a decision, a dream, or even a fear. Hand it over to Him, one small step at a time. Trusting God, even when it feels scary, builds the confidence and faith to trust Him more.

6. **Stay Connected to His Word Daily:** Keep Scripture visible— on your phone, in your workspace, or on your bathroom mirror. A verse like **1 Peter 1:8-9** can be a lifeline in tough moments. The more you stay in His Word, the more you'll see your faith grow naturally.

God's faithfulness assures us that He has a good plan for our lives, allowing us to experience incredible and flourishing joy and purpose. As we mature in our understanding of His faithfulness, we grow in our own confident faith in Him.

Reflection and Discussion Questions:

As we meditate on this week's study verses: **1 Peter 1:8-9, Hebrews 11:1, Psalm 16:11, Jeremiah 29:11, Psalms 62:8, and Philippians 1:25, what common theme** is the Lord showing or revealing to you about joy?

_____

_____

What do you think the Lord Jesus **would like you to understand from these verses** about His joy and how it fills, strengthens, and transforms the lives of those who love and obey Him?

_____

_____

Application:

What are **two (2) practical ways** we can apply what we have studied to our lives this coming week? You can choose from the list of suggestions or use your own.

1._____

_____

2._____

_____

What good things do you expect to happen as we apply these truths to our lives?

1._____

_____

2._____

_____

Simple Prayer:

Lord, thank you for revealing your goodness, strength, and ever-present presence to us. As we walk through this week, help us see you more clearly, remember your past goodness, and walk closer to you. In Jesus' name, we pray. Amen.

Chapter Four

Unquenchable Joy-Week 4

*"The Lord is my strength and my shield; my heart
trusts in him, and he helps me. **My heart leaps for joy,
and with my song, I praise him.***"
Psalm 28:7

Study and Meditation for the Week: Trust

Trusting in God's sovereignty and goodness is an anchor for our hearts, especially when life feels chaotic and uncertain. Trust has a unique way of replacing anxiety with peace and making room for joy to take root and thrive. When we lean into trust, we find renewed energy and enthusiasm that helps us move forward, even when the path ahead isn't clear. Trusting God means releasing our worries and fears into His capable hands and believing that He has a plan for our lives and that His plans are truly good, a principle we looked at last week.

Proverbs 3:5-6 says, **"Trust in the Lord with all your heart and lean not on your own understanding; in all your ways submit to him, and he will make your paths straight."** These words remind us that trusting God isn't just a feeling; it's an action. It's an intentional decision to let go of trying to figure everything out on our own and instead place our confidence in His wisdom and guidance. I know firsthand how tempting it is to rely on my own understanding, but when I pause and say, "God, I trust You," there's an undeniable peace that follows. It's the kind of peace that only comes from knowing that He's got this—even if I don't.

Psalm 28:7 beautifully describes this: "**The Lord is my strength and my shield; my heart trusts in him, and he helps me. My heart leaps for joy, and with my song, I praise him.**" Here, we see the direct link between trust and joy. When we trust God, we don't just find calm; we find strength and joy. Trust becomes the fuel that lights up our spirit, reminding us that we're not walking this journey alone.

Psalm 52:8 says, "**But I am like an olive tree flourishing in the house of God; I trust in God's unfailing love for ever and ever.**" Think about that image—an olive tree, strong and flourishing. That's what happens when we root our trust in God's love. No matter what storms come, we can remain steadfast and even thrive because we're grounded in His enduring, unchanging love. Trusting God doesn't mean life will be free from challenges, but we can withstand them gracefully and confidently.

I live in an area surrounded by magnificent olive groves; these trees withstand intense storms with little, if any, damage. With their silvery foliage, rugged trunks, and clusters of fragrant white flowers in spring, these distinctive trees remain green and beautiful year-round, bearing rich and beneficial fruit.

Psalm 62:8 encourages us further: "**Trust in him at all times, you people; pour out your hearts to him, for God is our refuge.**" Trusting God is more than a quiet assurance; it's also an active dialogue. When we pour out our hearts—our worries, hopes, fears, and joys to Him, we're reminded that God is not just a distant king; He's our father, our refuge, a safe place where we can be real. And when we trust Him like this, joy fills our hearts because we know that whatever we're facing, He's holding us securely in His arms of love.

Psalm 91:2 says, **"I will say of the Lord, 'He is my refuge and my fortress, my God, in whom I trust."** This declaration is powerful because it affirms that trust is more than a thought—it's a proclamation. Speaking out that trust reinforces it in our hearts and minds. I've found that when I say out loud, "God, I trust You," it becomes a reminder not just for my head but for my heart, solidifying that trust and allowing peace to replace worry.

So, how do we bring this kind of trust into our everyday lives? Here are some practical steps:

1. **Start Your Day by Acknowledging God's Control:** Before jumping into the busyness of the day, take a moment to remind yourself, "God, today is in Your hands." This small habit shifts our mindset from self-reliance to trust and purpose.

2. **Replace Worry with Prayer:** When you catch yourself spiraling with "what ifs," pause and turn those worries into prayers. **Psalm 62:8** invites us to pour out our hearts to Him because He is our refuge. Use those moments of anxiety as reminders to reconnect with God.

3. **Speak Trust Out Loud:** Whether it's saying, "God, I trust You," or declaring **Psalm 91:2**, speaking your trust reinforces it. It's a small action that can make a big difference in shifting from fear to faith.

4. **Lean on Scriptures and Affirmations:** Carry verses like **Proverbs 3:5-6** and **Psalm 52:8** with you. Write them on sticky notes, keep them as your phone background, or say them during your quiet time. Let these reminders be lifelines on tough days.

When we trust God with our worries and choose to believe in His goodness, we can face life with confidence that brings peace and joy. We're reminded that while we may not control every twist and turn, the One who holds our future is faithful and true. Trusting in Him is what lets us walk forward not just with hope but with an unquenchable joy that endures.

Reflection and Discussion Questions:

As we meditate on this week's study verses, **Psalm 28:7, Proverbs 3:5-6, Psalm 28:7, Psalm 52:8, Psalm 62:8,** and **Psalm 91:2, what common theme** is the Lord showing or revealing to you about joy?

_____

_____

What do you think the Lord Jesus **would like you to understand from these verses** about His joy and how it fills, strengthens, and transforms the lives of those who love and obey Him?

_____

_____

Application:

What are **two (2) practical ways** we can apply what we have studied to our lives this coming week? You can choose from the list we discussed or create some of your own to try.

1._____

_____

2._____

_____

What do you think the Lord Jesus **would like you to understand from these verses** about His joy and how it completely fills, strengthens, and transforms the lives of those who love and obey Him?

1._____

_____

2._____

_____

Simple Prayer:

Lord, we put our trust in you, believing your plans for us are good and that you will never leave our side. Help us to remember your love and your promises. May our trust be unwavering, and may it inspire others to seek your love and guidance. In Jesus' name, we pray. Amen.

Chapter Five

Unquenchable Joy-Week 5

*"The precepts of the Lord are right, **giving joy to the heart**. The commands of the Lord are radiant, giving light to the eyes."* **Psalm 19:8**

Study and Meditation for the Week: Obedience

Obedience to God's commandments is not a restrictive duty; it's the road to true, unquenchable joy. Sometimes, "obedience" gets a bad reputation, making us think of rules, regulations, or limitations. But when we see it through the lens of God's love and wisdom, it changes everything. Jesus made it clear in **John 15:10-11** when He said, **"If you keep my commands, you will remain in my love, just as I have kept my Father's commands and remain in his love. I have told you this so that my joy may be in you and that your joy may be complete."** That's powerful.

He's not asking us to follow Him for the sake of rigid compliance; He's inviting us into a life where His joy becomes ours, and it's complete—whole, lacking nothing.

Psalm 119:111 echoes this beautifully: **"Your statutes are my heritage forever; they are the joy of my heart."** A deep contentment comes from living in step with God's word. The psalmist calls God's commands a "heritage," something cherished and passed down, highlighting that God's ways are a gift meant to bring us joy. It's not just about rules but about living in a way that aligns with God's good plans for us. When we choose obedience, we're choosing to live out the purpose He's designed for us, and with that comes a sense of fulfillment and joy that goes far beyond what the world offers.

Psalm 19:8 also brings this to light: **"The precepts of the Lord are right, giving joy to the heart. The commands of the Lord are radiant, giving light to the eyes."** Here, joy is directly tied to following God's guidelines, which light up our path and bring clarity to our lives. Think about how good it feels when you know you're on the right track, even if the road is challenging. That's what obedience to God brings—a deep, settled joy that doesn't depend on everything going perfectly but on knowing you're walking in the light of God's truth.

And this kind of joy, the kind that comes from following God's ways, isn't fragile. It's resilient. **James 1:2-3** tells us, **"Consider it pure joy, my brothers and sisters, whenever you face trials of many kinds, because you know that the testing of your faith produces perseverance."** This verse flips the script on how we usually think about trials. It's not saying to pretend tough times are fun or easy but to recognize that even in hardship, joy can exist. Why? Because those challenges are building perseverance, strengthening our faith, and drawing us closer to God. Even in difficult times, obedience becomes a path where joy is found, not lost.

So, how do we put this kind of joyful obedience into practice? It starts with seeing God's commandments not as a list of rules but as a guide to the life He knows is best for us. Here are some practical steps to get there:

1. **Take Time to Know His Word:** Joy in obedience starts with understanding what God's asking of us. Spend time reading scripture, focusing on verses like **John 15:10-11**, and asking God to show you how His commands are a pathway to joy. Reflect on how His teachings connect with your life and the moments where following them has brought you peace or clarity.

2. **Start Small and Stay Consistent:** Obedience doesn't have to mean huge, life-altering changes all at once. It can start with small, daily choices. It could be choosing patience when you're frustrated or speaking the truth even when it's uncomfortable. Each small act of obedience strengthens our joy and connection to God.

3. **Remember Past Faithfulness: Psalm 119:111** and **Psalm 19:8** remind us that God's commands bring joy and light. Reflect on past moments where obeying God led to blessings, peace, or growth. Use those memories as encouragement when you face situations that make obedience feel hard or counterintuitive.

4. **Trust in the Outcome, Even When It's Unclear: Psalm 62:8** says, **"Trust in him at all times, you people; pour out your hearts to him, for God is our refuge."** Sometimes, following God's commands won't make immediate sense or feel comfortable. In those moments, trust that God sees the bigger picture. Obedience is an act of trust that He's working for your good, even if you don't see it right away.

5. **Keep Joy at the Center:** Remind yourself of the promise in **John 15:11**—that Jesus' goal is for His joy to be in us and for our joy to be complete. This isn't about following rules with a dull heart but embracing them happily with the understanding that they lead to a deeper, lasting joy.

Obedience to God's precepts invites us into a deeper relationship where His joy becomes our joy, not just in the easy times but even when life tests us. It's not about perfection; it's about choosing, step by step, day by day, to trust Him and align our actions with His will. When we do, we'll find that joy isn't something we chase—it's something that grows within us, resilient and unwavering.

Reflection and Discussion Questions:

As we meditate on this week's study verses: **Psalm 119:111, Psalm 19:8, John 15:10-11, John 15:10-11,** and **James 1:2-3 what common theme** is the Lord showing or revealing to you about joy?

_____

_____

What do you think the Lord Jesus **would like you to understand from these verses** about His joy and how it fills, strengthens, and transforms the lives of those who love and obey Him?

_____

_____

Application:

What are **two (2) practical ways** we can apply what we have studied to our lives this coming week? You can choose from the list we discussed or create some of your own to try.

1._____

_____

2._____

_____

What good things do you expect to happen as we apply these truths to our lives?

1._____

_____

2._____

_____

Simple Prayer:

Father, we are grateful for your love and guidance, and we want to follow your teachings with joyful hearts. Help us to find happiness in doing what is right and in living a life that honors you. May our obedience to your ways bring us closer to you each day. In Jesus' name, we pray. Amen.

Chapter Six

Unquenchable Joy-Week 6

*"You make known to me the path of life; in your presence there is **fullness of joy**."* **Psalm 16:11**

Study and Meditation for the Week: God's Presence

God's presence is our steadfast anchor, especially when life feels overwhelming and uncertain. You know those times when everything seems chaotic, and you feel like you are running on empty? In those moments, seeking the presence of God fills us with peace and joy that the world can't offer. Spending time with Him isn't just a "nice-to-have"—it's essential. Whether we're taking a few minutes to pray, read a verse, or sing our hearts out in worship, those moments with God can refresh our spirits and remind us of His unfailing love and faithfulness.

Psalm 16:11 puts it so beautifully: **"You make known to me the path of life; in your presence, there is fullness of joy; at your right hand are pleasures forevermore."** Think about that—fullness of joy! Not just a little happiness but joy that fills every part of us. When we make time to be in God's presence, we're reminded that He is the source of true joy, not our circumstances or fleeting successes.

And it's not just a one-time thing. **Psalm 21:6** says, **"Surely you have granted him unending blessings and made him glad with the joy of your presence."** It's a continuous joy, not just here today and gone tomorrow. When life drains us or throws us curveballs, going back to God refills that well of joy. His presence becomes our safe place, a constant we can rely on. His presence causes us to overflow, spilling out to others.

The early followers of Jesus knew this, and it's captured perfectly in **Acts 2:28: "You have made known to me the paths of life; you will fill me with joy in your presence."** Even when life was tough, and they faced real challenges, they found joy by staying close to God and holding on to His promises. It reminds me that real and lasting joy is still possible even when my world feels upside down because His presence doesn't change.

Job understood this, too, even during the most challenging times of his life. **Job 33:26** says, **"Then that person can pray to God and find favor with him; they will see God's face and shout for joy; he will restore them to full well-being."** If Job, with everything he had gone through, could find joy by turning to God, then so can we. It's a reminder that no matter how deep our struggles go, spending time with God can restore us and bring joy that doesn't make sense by the world's standards.

Psalm 89:15-16 hits home with, **"Blessed are those who have learned to acclaim you, who walk in the light of your presence, Lord. They rejoice in your name all day long; they celebrate your righteousness."** Walking in God's light doesn't mean life will be perfect, but it does mean we have a source of joy and strength that's always there. When we focus on Him and make time to be in His presence, joy can't help but overflow into our lives.

So, how can we make this practical, stay connected to God's presence, and keep that joy alive?

1. **Find Your Quiet Moments with God:** Maybe it's in the early morning before the chaos starts or late at night when the house is quiet. Just take a few minutes to sit with God. Read a verse like **Psalm 16:11** or **Acts 2:28**, and let it sink in. Talk to Him about your day or just sit and listen. The more we do this, the more we'll feel that joy bubbling up inside.

2. **Bring Worship Into Your Day:** Worship isn't just for Sunday mornings. Play your favorite worship songs while driving, cooking, or doing chores. Sing along, or just let the music remind you of God's goodness. **Psalm 89:15-16** tells us that those who walk in His light rejoice all day—worship helps keep that light in our hearts.

3. **Pray Throughout the Day:** Don't save prayer for the "big" moments. Whisper prayers of gratitude when something good happens, or ask for help when you're stressed. **Psalm 62:8** says, **"Trust in him at all times, you people; pour out your hearts to him, for God is our refuge."** Prayer is how we stay close to Him and keep that connection strong.

4. **Stay Rooted in His Word:** Make scripture a regular part of your life. Keep verses like **Psalm 28:7** nearby: **"The Lord is my strength and my shield; my heart trusts in him, and he helps me. My heart leaps for joy, and with my song, I praise him."** Let those words remind you that God's presence is where joy begins.

When we make time for God's presence, we're not just going through the motions. We're filling up on something that lifts us up, calms our worries, and fills us with joy that's deeper than anything we could find on our own. No matter what's going on, we can hold onto that joy, knowing God is walking with us through it all.

Reflection and Discussion Questions:

As we meditate on this week's study verses: **Psalm 16:11, Psalm 21:6, Acts 2:28, Job 33:26,** and **Psalm 89:15-16, what common theme** is the Lord showing or revealing to you about joy?

_____

_____

What do you think the Lord Jesus **would like you to understand from these verses** about His joy and how it completely fills, strengthens, and transforms the lives of those who love and obey Him?

_____

_____

Application:

Where do you find your quiet times with God?

1._____

_____

2._____

_____

What good things do you expect to happen as we apply these truths to our lives?

1._____

_____

2._____

_____

Simple Prayer:

Dear Lord, we find so much happiness in knowing that you are always with us and that your love never ends. Help us to feel your presence in our daily lives and to find joy in the simple things that remind us of your love. May our hearts be filled with your peace and happiness, and may we share that joy with others. In Jesus' name, we pray. Amen.

Chapter Seven

Unquenchable Joy-Week 7

"That which we have seen and heard we declare to you,
that you also may have fellowship with us; and truly
our fellowship is with the Father and with His Son, Jesus
*Christ. And these things write we unto you, that **your***
joy may be full. *"* **1 John 1:3-4**

Study and Meditation for the Week: Community

The fellowship and support of a loving, faith-filled church community are essential for our walk with God. We need each other—not just for the big moments, but for the everyday ups and downs that come with life. **Galatians 6:2** says, **"Carry each other's burdens, and in this way, you will fulfill the law of Christ."** There's something so powerful about sharing what we're going through with people who care about us and want to lift us up. When we let others come alongside us in our struggles, we find a kind of strength and joy that's hard to find on our own. When we can be the needed helping hand and support someone else needs, it increases our joy. We weren't meant to do this life alone; we were created to live in community.

Psalm 122:1 captures the joy of being part of a faith community or church body: "I rejoiced with those who said to me, **"Let us go to the house of the Lord."** A unique kind of happiness comes from gathering with others who share your faith, whether it's worshiping together, sharing testimonies, or just being in the same space, knowing you're all there for the same reason—to seek God and support one another. That shared experience fills us with joy and strengthens our spirits. It's a reminder that we are part of something bigger than ourselves, and we're not alone. The joy of community is a powerful force that enriches our lives.

1 John 1:3-4 talks about this sense of connection: **"We proclaim to you what we have seen and heard, so that you also may have fellowship with us. And our fellowship is with the Father and His Son, Jesus Christ. We write this to make your joy complete."** There's a joy that comes from sharing what God has done in our lives with others and hearing their stories, too. That back-and-forth sharing deepens our faith and makes our joy fuller. When we're in fellowship, it's not just about being together; it's about experiencing God together.

Paul understood the importance of this when he wrote in **Philippians 2:2, "Then make my joy complete by being like-minded, having the same love, being one in spirit and of one mind."** There's joy in unity, in knowing that we're all on this journey together, supporting one another and growing in love. It's about being focused on the same goal—living out God's love and truth. That kind of unity of a shared goal fills our hearts and reminds us that we're stronger together. Unity in a church community is not just a concept; it's a reality that we can all experience and benefit from.

The early church knew the power of this kind of community well. **Acts 2:46-47** gives us a beautiful picture of what life in the early church faith community looked like: **"Every day they continued to meet together in the temple courts. They broke bread in their homes and ate together with glad and sincere hearts, praising God and enjoying the favor of all the people. And the Lord added to their number daily those who were being saved."** They shared meals, spent time together, and lifted each other up, and because of that, they experienced a joy that was both sincere and deep. Their faith community wasn't just about meeting needs but celebrating life and faith together.

2 Corinthians 13:11 reminds us to strive for a loving community like a family: **"Finally, brothers and sisters, rejoice! Strive for full restoration, encourage one another, be of one mind, live in peace. And the God of love and peace will be with you."** Encouragement, unity, and peace bring joy because they reflect God's presence among us. When we take the time to support and uplift each other, we experience a tangible sense of God's love working through us and within us.

So, how do we make this supportive community part of our lives?

1. **Show Up Regularly:** Make it a habit to be part of your church's gatherings or small groups. Just showing up consistently makes a difference and helps build that sense of connection. Like **Psalm 122:1** says, find joy in being with others who are there to seek God. Your regular participation is a testament to your commitment and engagement in the community.

2. **Be Open and Vulnerable:** It's easy to put up walls and pretend we're doing fine, but genuine fellowship comes when we're honest about our struggles. Let others in, and be willing to carry their burdens, too. **Galatians 6:2** encourages us to share the load, and there's joy in knowing we're helping each other through life.

3. **Celebrate Together:** Don't just share the tough times; share the good ones, too! **Acts 2:46-47** shows that joy is found in both the everyday moments and the big celebrations. Host a dinner, visit someone who is homebound, or celebrate a

friend's answered prayer. These moments create joy that ripples through the whole church community.

4. **Encourage One Another:** Be intentional about lifting others up. Whether it's a quick text, a phone call, or a word of encouragement after church, these gestures go a long way. **Philippians 2:2** reminds us that joy comes when we're unified and looking out for each other.

5. **Serve Together:** Find ways to serve your community or those in need as a group. A special kind of joy comes from working side by side, helping others, and seeing the impact you can make together. It bonds people and reminds us why we're here—to love God and love others. This shared purpose and the joy of making a difference together is fulfilling. Being part of a faith community or church isn't just about having people to lean on; it's about sharing life, faith, and joy with one another.

Reflection and Discussion Questions:

As we meditate on this week's study verses, **1 John 1:3-4, Galatians 6:2, Psalm 122:1, Acts 2:46-47, Philippians 2:2, and 2 Corinthians 13:11, what common theme** is the Lord showing or revealing to you about joy?

_____

_____

What do you think the Lord Jesus **would like you to understand from these verses** about His joy and how it fills, strengthens, and transforms the lives of those who love and obey Him?

_____

_____

Application:

What are **two (2) practical ways** we can apply what we have studied to our lives this coming week? You can choose from the list we discussed or create some of your own to try.

1._____

_____

2._____

_____

What good things do you expect to happen as we apply these truths to our lives?

1._____

_____

2._____

_____

Simple Prayer:

Lord, we are so thankful for the community of believers that you have given us, and the joy we find in being part of your family. Help us to support and encourage one another, and to find strength in the love and friendship we share. May our unity and joy be a witness to the world of your love and grace. We pray in Jesus' name. Amen.

Chapter Eight

Unquenchable Joy-Week 8

*"It is good to give thanks to the Lord and to sing praises
to Your name, O Most High, to declare Your
lovingkindness in the morning, and Your faithfulness
every night."* **Psalm 92:1-2**

Study and Meditation for the Week: Daily Devotion

Daily devotion isn't just a box to check off in our daily schedule or a chore; it's a lifeline. I've found that the more I prioritize this time, the more grounded and connected I feel and the more successful I am in reaching my goals with less stress. Spending time in God's Word and daily prayer deepens our relationship with Jesus and roots us in His promises. It's not about having a perfect setup or schedule but about making time to really meet with God. That intentional practice shapes how we face the day, filling us with peace, joy, and purpose.

Psalm 143:8 says, **"Let the morning bring me word of your unfailing love, for I have put my trust in you. Show me the way I should go, for to you I entrust my life."** There's something so special about mornings. It's like hitting a reset button, a moment when the world is still quiet, and we can dedicate ourselves to God before the demands of the day begin. I love how David speaks to the fresh hope and trust that mornings bring. When we start our day by reading scripture and talking to God, we're reminded of His unfailing love and the guidance He's ready to offer. It sets the tone for everything that follows.

But maybe mornings aren't your thing, and that's okay. The most important part is making the time, whether that's in the morning, afternoon, or evening. I've found that creating a dedicated space helps. It could be a cozy corner with a comfy chair, a Bible, and maybe even a journal to write down prayers or reflections. Some people find peace in a spot outside, like a quiet place on a porch, deck, or garden. Regardless of where it is, having a space you look forward to retreating to meet with God makes it easier to incorporate that dedicated time with God into your daily life.

Psalm 92:1-2 reminds us, "**It is good to praise the Lord and make music to your name, O Most High, proclaiming your love in the morning and your faithfulness at night.**" This verse is such a beautiful reminder that time with God isn't just for the start of the day. There's value in evening devotions, too, where we can reflect on our day, thank Him for His faithfulness, and ask for insight on how the day went. I've had some of the most meaningful moments in those quiet evening prayers, asking, "Lord, is there anything I should have done differently today? How can I do better tomorrow?" It's not about feeling guilty or beating ourselves up; it's about growing and being open to His gentle guidance so we can continuously improve in our walk and get closer to Him.

Mark 1:35 gives us a glimpse into Jesus' own routine: "**Very early in the morning, while it was still dark, Jesus got up, left the house, and went off to a solitary place, where he prayed.**" If Jesus, who was fully God and fully man, made time to step away from everything to pray, how much more do we need that time? It doesn't have to be elaborate. Sometimes, I'd go out to my car during my lunch break to get a few minutes alone with God. In the middle of a busy, hectic day filled with work and kids, that little break became a sanctuary. It was where I could pause, breathe, and remember God was right there with me. Yours may be the drive home from work, but as long as it provides time for you and God to meet, it's a daily routine worth establishing.

Psalm 43:4 says, **"Then I will go to the altar of God, to God, my joy and my delight."** That's what our quiet time becomes—an altar where we meet with God, our source of joy and delight. Even if all we can manage is 10 minutes, those minutes can transform our mindset and remind us who holds our day in His hands.

Here are some suggestions to think about that may help you make daily devotion a more consistent and meaningful part of your life:

1. **Set an Intention:** Decide what time works best for you and commit to it. Maybe it's first thing in the morning with your coffee or before bed when the house is quiet. **Psalm 143:8** encourages us to start our day with His love, but any time you choose is valuable as long as you show up.

2. **Create Your Sacred Space:** Pick a spot that feels peaceful to you. Whether it's a chair by the window, a corner in your room, or even your car at lunchtime, setting aside a place helps your mind and heart prepare to meet with God.

3. **Keep It Simple:** Your devotion time doesn't have to be long or complicated. Start by reading a Psalm or a short passage, like **Psalm 92:1-2**, and spend a few minutes praying about whatever is on your heart. Ask God to guide your day or reflect on what He's already done.

4. **Stay Flexible:** Life happens, and some days will be harder to manage than others. If you miss your morning devotion, find a quiet moment later in the day. **Mark 1:35** shows us that even Jesus adapted His schedule to make space for God.

5. **Reflect and Grow:** At the end of the day, take a moment for an evening devotion. Use it to thank God for His faithfulness, like the Psalmist in **Psalm 92:2**, and to ask Him if there's anything you need to learn from that day. It's a chance to reset and prepare for the next day with Him at the center.

Daily devotion isn't about perfection; it's about consistency and connection. Whether you have a whole hour or just a few stolen minutes in a busy day, each moment you spend with God matters. It fills you with His peace, grounds you in His promises, and fills your life with unquenchable joy, peace, and power through the Holy Spirit.

Reflection and Discussion Questions:

As we meditate on this week's study verses: **Psalm 143:8, Psalms 92:1-2, Psalm 43:4, Psalm 143:8,** and **Mark 1:35, what common theme** is the Lord showing or revealing to you about joy?

_____

_____

What do you think the Lord Jesus **would like you to understand from these verses** about His joy and how it completely fills, strengthens, and transforms the lives of those who love and obey Him?

_____

_____

Application:

What are **two (2) practical ways** we can apply what we have studied to our lives this coming week? You can choose from the list of suggestions or come up with your own.

1._____

_____

2._____

_____

What good things do you expect to happen as we apply these truths to our lives?

1._____

_____

2._____

_____

Simple Prayer:

Dear Lord, we love starting our day with you, talking to you, and learning from your Word. Help us to make time for daily devotion and prayer and to find joy in growing closer to you. May our quiet moments with you fill our hearts with peace, happiness, and a deeper understanding of your love for us. In Jesus' name, we pray. Amen.

Chapter Nine

Unquenchable Joy-Week 9

"I will be glad and rejoice in You; I will sing praise to Your name, O Most High." **Psalm 9:2**

Study and Meditation for the Week: Worship

Worship is more than just singing songs on a Sunday morning—it's a declaration of who God is and an acknowledgment of His unmatched greatness. It's our way of expressing awe, respect, honor, and devotion to the One who stands above all, the Creator of the heavens and the earth, the One who spoke and brought everything into being. When we worship, we open ourselves to experience His greatness, letting it flow into every corner of our lives as we stand in awe of the One who was, is, and always will be. Worship shifts us into perfect alignment with God as we glorify the only One truly deserving of our praise and adoration.

Psalm 9:2 puts it perfectly: **"I will be glad and rejoice in you; I will sing the praises of your name, O Most High."** There's a joy that bubbles up when we praise God, a joy that it's not only humans that have to seek the facts to make sure that the research is available that can't help but spill over into every part of our day. Worship fuels this joy, taking us beyond our circumstances and helping us focus on God's unchanging nature. When life feels uncertain or overwhelming, worship reminds us who is truly in control, bringing peace and a fresh perspective.

Isaiah 55:12 says, **"You will go out in joy and be led forth in peace; the mountains and hills will burst into song before you, and all the trees of the field will clap their hands."** There's an energy in worship that's contagious. It's as if creation itself joins in, celebrating the Creator. We tap into that same joy and peace when we worship, allowing it to overflow into our everyday lives. And it doesn't always have to be loud or extravagant—sometimes worship is found in quiet moments where we reflect on His goodness and let gratitude fill our hearts.

Psalm 63:3-4 resonates deeply with me: **"Because your love is better than life, my lips will glorify you. I will praise you as long as I live, and I will lift up my hands in your name."** This kind of worship is personal and heartfelt. It's the moment when you're alone, maybe in the middle of your day, and you just pause to thank God for His love. I've had moments where I was driving or just sitting in my room, and something stirred in me to lift my hands and say, "Thank you, God, for being who You are." Those moments are powerful, not because of how they look but because they shift our focus back to Him.

Psalm 33:3 invites us to **"Sing to him a new song; play skillfully, and shout for joy."** Worship can be creative and joyful, incorporating music, art, and even dance. Sometimes, it's in writing a poem or journaling about God's faithfulness. Other times, it's turning up worship music and singing at the top of your lungs, even if it's just you in the room. Don't worry about how it sounds—God's not grading us on performance. He cares that it's coming from our hearts.

Psalm 68:4 encourages us to **"Sing to God, sing in praise of his name, extol him who rides on the clouds; rejoice before him— his name is the Lord."** This verse reminds me that worship is an invitation to rejoice, to celebrate who God is and what He's done. Sometimes, that looks like dancing around the house with your kids or having a moment of spontaneous praise. Other times, it's a more solemn moment of bowing your head and whispering thanks. Whatever form it takes, worship reconnects us to God's heart.

Psalm 98:4-6 captures the full range of worship: **"Shout for joy to the Lord, all the earth, burst into jubilant song with music; make music to the Lord with the harp, with the harp and the sound of singing, with trumpets and the blast of the ram's horn—shout for joy before the Lord, the King."** The people of Israel worshiped with everything they had—songs, instruments, and even shouting. It was an all-in moment of showing God their devotion. And we can do the same today in our own ways.

So, how can we make worship a regular, meaningful part of our daily lives? Here are a few ideas:

1. **Start Your Day with Worship:** Begin your morning with a worship song or a few moments of quiet reflection. **Psalm 143:8** says, **"Let the morning bring me word of your unfailing love, for I have put my trust in you."** Let your first thoughts of the day be about His love and faithfulness. Even if it's just a quick prayer or a song as you're getting ready, it sets the tone for the day.

2. **Incorporate Music:** Create a playlist of your favorite worship songs and listen to them while you're driving, cooking, or working. Singing along or just letting the music fill the space can lift your spirit, invite the Holy Spirit, and bring God's

presence, as **Psalm 22:3** reminds us, **"He inhabits the praise of His people."**

3. **Express Your Worship Through Creativity:** Write a poem, paint a picture, or journal about what God's been doing in your life. **Psalm 33:3** reminds us that worship can be creative. Use the gifts you have to praise Him in your own unique way.

4. **Make Room for Quiet Worship:** Take a moment in the evening to sit in silence, reflecting on God's goodness and faithfulness from the day. **Psalm 63:3-4** encourages us to lift our hands and praise Him, even in these quiet, private moments.

5. **Join in Community Worship:** Worship is powerful when we're alone, but there's something special about joining with others. Find ways to worship with friends or your church community, whether in person or through an online service. The shared experience amplifies the joy and brings us closer together.

Worship isn't just an action; it's a heart posture. It's choosing to focus on God's greatness and letting that awe change how we see everything around us. When we make worship a part of our daily routine, we invite His presence into our day, filling us with joy and a deeper awareness of His love. Let's make worship a habit that transforms us from the inside out.

Reflection and Discussion Questions:

As we meditate on this week's study verses: **Psalm 9:2, Isaiah 55:12, Psalm 63:3-4, Psalm 33:3, Psalm 68:4, Psalm 98:4-6, Psalm 143:8,** and

Psalm 22:3, what common theme is the Lord showing or revealing to you about joy?

_____

_____

What do you think the Lord Jesus **would like you to understand from these verses** about His joy and how it completely fills, strengthens, and transforms the lives of those who love and obey Him?

_____

_____

Application:

What are **two (2) practical ways** we can apply what we have studied to our lives this coming week?

1._____

_____

2._____

_____

What good things do you expect to happen as we apply these truths to our lives?

1._____

_____

2._____

Simple Prayer:

God, we love to sing your praises and to worship you with all our hearts. Help us to find true joy in celebrating your goodness. May our worship be a beautiful offering to you, and may it bring us closer to you and to each other. In Jesus' name, we pray. Amen.

Chapter Ten

Unquenchable Joy-Week 10

*"I have told you this so that my joy may be in you and that **your joy may be complete.**"* **John 15:11**

Study and Meditation for the Week: Service

Serving the Lord and others isn't just something we should do—it's a source of incredible joy in our lives. The Bible teaches us that in God's kingdom, the highest position is that of a servant. Serving isn't about obligation or recognition; it's about stepping into a role that reflects Jesus' own heart. And what's amazing is that when we serve, we discover a deep, lasting joy that shifts our perspective and fills our lives with purpose.

Psalm 100:2 encourages us to **"Worship the Lord with gladness; come before him with joyful songs."** This verse reminds us when we view serving as an act of worship it isn't meant to be done out of a sense of duty or obligation but with gladness. When we serve with joy, it transforms the experience entirely. We move from just doing something because we feel we *have* to do it because we *get* to. There's a big difference, and that shift can be life-changing.

It reminds us that when we look beyond our struggles to serve others, our problems don't feel as daunting. There's joy in stepping out of our world and into someone else's to make a difference. Sometimes, serving can feel like one more thing on our already packed to-do list, but I've learned that the deepest joy is often when we're stretched. It's in the unexpected smile from a stranger or the genuine "thank you" from a friend that we feel the impact of what we're doing. Serving reminds us that life isn't just about us; it's about being part of God's bigger plan and showing His love in action.

Let's be honest—there are days when we don't feel like serving because we're tired or overwhelmed. But even then, God meets us in that space. Often, in those moments when we push past our own comfort and personal agendas, we experience the most joy and see God working in unexpected ways.

Psalm 35:27 says, **"May those who delight in my vindication shout for joy and gladness; may they always say, 'The Lord be exalted, who delights in the well-being of his servant.'"** God takes joy in our well-being and designed us to find joy in serving others. It's a beautiful cycle—when we serve, we feel joy, and that joy honors God. It's like fueling a fire that makes our spirits burn brighter.

Jesus talked about this in **John 15:11, "I have told you this so that my joy may be in you and that your joy may be complete."** Jesus wants His joy to be in us, and serving others is one way we step into that complete joy. Think about how He spent His time on earth. He washed feet, fed the hungry, healed the sick, and reached out to those who were overlooked. Jesus didn't come to be served but to serve, and when we follow His example, we tap into a joy that's fulfilling and contagious.

Serving also helps us stay grounded and focused on what truly matters. **1 Corinthians 15:58** encourages us with these words: **"Therefore, my**

dear brothers and sisters, stand firm. Let nothing move you. Always give yourselves fully to the work of the Lord, because you know that your labor in the Lord is not in vain." We might not always see immediate results when we serve, but God assures us that our work for Him is never wasted. Every act of kindness, every moment spent helping someone else, adds up in ways we might not see but are always seen by God.

Psalm 34:22 says, **"The Lord will rescue his servants; no one who takes refuge in him will be condemned."** Serving God and others isn't just about the joy it brings—it's also about trusting that as we pour out, God is pouring His joy into us and protecting us as His servants. He sees when we serve Him and others with genuine hearts, and He's faithful to be our refuge, strength, and source of our joy.

So, how do we make serving a part of our everyday lives? Here are some relatable and practical steps:

1. **Look for Simple Opportunities:** Serving doesn't have to be a grand gesture. It can be as simple as helping a neighbor with their groceries, calling a friend who's going through a tough time, or volunteering a couple of hours at a local charity. These small acts can bring as much joy as the big ones. For instance, you could offer to walk your neighbor's dog when they're busy or cook a meal for a friend who's feeling under the weather. These seemingly small acts can have a big impact on someone's day.

2. **Use Your Gifts:** God has given each of us unique talents and abilities. You may be great at organizing, baking, teaching, or listening. Use those gifts to serve others. There's joy in knowing you're using what God has put inside of you to bless someone else, and in doing so, you bring a unique and valuable contribution to the world.

3. **Make It a Family Affair:** Serving together as a family or with friends adds a special layer of joy. Whether it's cooking a meal for someone, volunteering at an event, or simply spending time helping a loved one, doing it together creates memories and bonds that last.

4. **Stay Present:** When you're serving, be fully there. It's easy to check off a box and move on, but the absolute joy comes when you take a moment to see the impact you're making and connect with the person you're helping. Those moments of eye contact, a shared laugh, or a heartfelt "thank you" remind you why serving is so special.

5. **Reflect on the Experience:** After serving, take a moment to thank God for the opportunity. **Psalm 100:2** reminds us to **"Serve the Lord with gladness; Come before His presence with singing."** So, thank Him for letting you be part of His work. Reflecting on how it impacted you helps you see the joy that comes from serving and makes you want to do it again. Consider journaling about your experience or sharing it with a friend. Reflecting on your service can help you see the joy it brought to others and yourself, reinforcing the value of serving.

Serving is about stepping out of our own world and stepping into someone else's. It's about realizing that we're part of something bigger and that our acts of kindness have ripple effects we may never fully see. But one thing is sure—when we serve, joy fills our hearts, and that joy not only lifts us up but glorifies the One who put that desire to serve within us. Even when it's hard, serving deepens our connection to Him and makes life richer and more meaningful. So, let's keep looking for those moments, big or small, and trust that every act counts and every bit of joy is worth it.

Reflection and Discussion Questions:

As we meditate on this week's study verses, **Psalm 100:2, Psalm 35:27, Psalm 34:22, John 15:11,** and **1 Corinthians 15:58, what common theme** is the Lord showing or revealing to you about joy?

_____

_____

What do you think the Lord Jesus **would like you to understand from these verses** about His joy and how it completely fills, strengthens, and transforms the lives of those who love and obey Him?

_____

_____

Application:

What are **two (2) practical ways** we can apply what we have studied to our lives this coming week? You can choose from the list of suggestions or two of your own.

1._____

_____

2._____

_____

What good things do you expect to happen as we apply these truths to our lives?

1._____

_____

2._____

_____

Simple Prayer:

Father, we are grateful for the opportunity to serve you and others. Help us to find joy in making a difference, no matter how small, and in showing your love through our actions. May our service be a blessing to those around us, and may it bring glory to your name. In Jesus' name, we pray. Amen.

Chapter Eleven

Unquenchable Joy-Week 11

"But those who wait on the Lord shall renew their strength; They shall mount up with wings like eagles; They shall run and not be weary; they shall walk and not faint." **Isaiah 40:31**

Study and Meditation for the Week: Self-Care

Prioritizing rest and self-care isn't just a luxury; it's a necessity. God designed us to need rest, and taking time to recharge—physically, emotionally, and spiritually—is essential and transformative. I can't count the number of times when my biggest struggles and discouragements have hit during periods when I am tired. But when I take a step back, rest, and allow myself to recharge, that discouragement lifts, and I feel more optimistic, energized, and ready to face what comes my way. Rest is truly restorative, and we all must prioritize it, even when life is busy and demanding of our time.

We need to remember that our bodies are temples of the Holy Spirit, as **1 Corinthians 6:19-20** tells us: **"Do you not know that your bodies are temples of the Holy Spirit, who is in you, whom you have received from God? You are not your own; you were bought at a price. Therefore, honor God with your bodies."**

When we care for our physical health—through rest, nourishing food, and self-care—we honor God. It's an act of stewardship, recognizing that He has given us these bodies as vessels for His work. And when we're feeling physically well, we're more capable of experiencing and sustaining joy. This includes maintaining a healthy mental state of focus.

Philippians 4:8 gives us a beautiful blueprint for what we should focus on: **"Finally, brothers and sisters, whatever is true, whatever is noble, whatever is right, whatever is pure, whatever is lovely, whatever is admirable—if anything is excellent or praiseworthy—think about such things."** Rest isn't just about sleep; rest can be found in taking a break from negativity and creating space to focus on what uplifts us and draws us closer to God. When we carve out moments to pause and reflect on His goodness, our hearts fill with peace and joy, knowing that He is with us in this journey of rest and self-care. Prioritizing rest and self-care is essential to true well-being; God designed us to need rest, and taking time to recharge physically, emotionally, and spiritually is essential for maintaining unquenchable joy.

Exodus 23:12 highlights the importance of rest, **"Six days do your work, but on the seventh day do not work, so that your ox and your donkey may rest and so that the slave born in your household and the foreigner living among you may be refreshed."** If God emphasized the importance of rest for people and even animals, how much more does He care for us taking the time to rest and recharge? It's not just about stopping work; or going on the long-awaited and anticipated vacation, where we can ditch our phones and disconnect; it's about allowing ourselves to breathe, reset, and find renewal on a daily basis.

Proverbs 3:24 reminds us of the gift of restful sleep: "**When you lie down, you will not be afraid; when you lie down, your sleep will be sweet.**" How many times have we tossed and turned, worrying about the next day? But when we commit our anxieties to God and prioritize rest, we're reminded that He's in control. A good night's sleep isn't just refreshing for the body; it's a balm for the soul. When we wake up rested, we're better equipped to embrace the day and all it holds with joy and confidence.

Isaiah 40:31 offers a promise for those who pause to wait on the Lord: "**But those who hope in the Lord will renew their strength. They will soar on wings like eagles; they will run and not grow weary; they will walk and not be faint.**" When we rest and spend time with God, we recharge physically and spiritually. We come out of those moments stronger, more refreshed, and ready to face whatever comes our way.

So, how can we prioritize rest and self-care in our busy lives? Here are a few ways that I've found helpful:

1. **Set Boundaries:** Protect your rest time by setting boundaries. It's easy to say "yes" to everything and everyone, but sometimes we need to say "no" to take care of ourselves. Create space in your schedule for downtime, and treat it as non-negotiable. This may be hard given your individual lives, but pray and ask the Lord to help you find that time and see His faithfulness in answering that prayer.

2. **Create a Relaxing Routine:** Whether it's a nightly ritual that involves reading a good book, listening to calming music, or taking a warm bath, find what helps you unwind and prepare for a restful sleep. **Proverbs 3:24** promises sweet sleep, and establishing a routine can help your body and mind prepare for

that rest. Experts agree that turning off all electronics at least an hour before bedtime helps our brains to quiet and prepare for restful sleep.

3. **Spend Time in Nature:** There's something about being outside that reconnects us with God's creation and brings a sense of peace. Even a short walk in the park or sitting in your backyard can be rejuvenating. Let nature remind you of God's vastness and His attention to detail—both in the world and in your life.

4. **Practice Mindful Moments with God:** Take short breaks throughout the day to pause and focus on God's presence. Breathe, pray, and let **Philippians 4:8** guide your thoughts to what is pure, lovely, and accurate. These moments don't have to be long, but they make a big difference. Research studies have shown that MRIs done on the brains of people who practice prayer revealed they have healthier brains than those who do not practice prayer. Technology is catching up with the truth of the Bible.

5. **Honor Your Physical Well-being:** Listen to your body. If you're tired, let yourself rest. If you're feeling tense, stretch or do a gentle workout. Remember, **1 Corinthians 6:19-20** says your body is a temple, and caring for it isn't selfish; it's necessary and stewardship of the precious gift you are to God.

Remember, rest and self-care aren't just for our benefit; they allow us to serve God and others with a joyful heart. When we prioritize taking care of ourselves, we're more joyful and better positioned to share that joy and serve from a place of abundance rather than exhaustion. Let's commit to making rest a regular part of our lives, trusting that when we do, we'll be strengthened, renewed, and filled with unquenchable joy. The benefits of establishing it as a priority for ourselves and others are beyond measure.

Reflection and Discussion Questions:

As we meditate on this week's study verses: **Isaiah 40:31, 1st Corinthians 6:19-20, Philippians 4:8, Exodus 23:12, Proverbs 3:24,** and **Isaiah 40:31, what common theme** is the Lord showing or revealing to you about joy?

_____

_____

What do you think the Lord Jesus **would like you to understand from these verses** about His joy and how it completely fills, strengthens, and transforms the lives of those who love and obey Him?

_____

_____

Application:

What are **two (2) practical ways** we can apply what we have studied to our lives this coming week? You can choose from the suggestions or use your own ideas.

1._____

_____

2._____

_____

What good things do you expect to happen as we apply these truths to our lives?

1._____

_____

2._____

_____

Simple Prayer:

Jesus, we know we are wonderfully made, and we want to take care of the bodies and minds you have given us. Help us to find joy in eating healthy, exercising, and getting enough rest so that we can serve you and others better. May our self-care be a way of honoring you and thanking you for the gift of life. In Jesus' name, we pray. Amen.

Chapter Twelve

Unquenchable Joy-Week 12

"Whatever you do, do it from the heart, as something done for the Lord and not for people."
Colossians 3:23

Study and Meditation for the Week: Creative Expression

Creative expression is a powerful way to connect with our Father, the ultimate creator, and experience the joy of the Holy Spirit. When we engage in creative activities, whether that's painting, music, writing, dance, gardening, sewing, or crafting, it can become an act of worship. It's not just about creating something beautiful; it's about allowing the Holy Spirit to guide and inspire us through the process.

I've felt that deep connection when I'm lost in writing, when my hands are busy crocheting a complex pattern, or when I'm pouring my heart into a quilt. It's as if God is right there with me, infusing the work with His presence and creativity, reminding me that He's the supreme Creator.

Proverbs 8:30-31 speaks to the joy and delight God Himself experiences in creation: **"Then I was constantly at his side. I was filled with delight day after day, rejoicing always in his presence, rejoicing in his whole world, and delighting in mankind."** If God rejoices in His creation, how much more should we delight in the creative abilities He's given us? When we take time to create, we're participating in that same divine joy, tapping into something profound and holy. It's a reminder that creativity isn't just a hobby; it's a reflection of being made in His image, where the spark of creation mirrors His infinite creativity.

Colossians 3:23 reminds us, **"Whatever you do, work at it with all your heart, as working for the Lord, not for human masters."** When we create with this mindset, our art, music, or crafts become offerings to God. It shifts our perspective from worrying about whether what we make is "good enough" to focusing on creating as an act of devotion. When I'm creating something with God at the forefront of my mind, I find a deeper sense of purpose and joy. It becomes less about the outcome and more about the journey, knowing I'm using my gifts to honor Him.

I love how **Exodus 35:31-33** describes God filling Bezalel with **"the Spirit of God, with wisdom, with understanding, with knowledge and with all kinds of skills—to make artistic designs for work in gold, silver, and bronze, to cut and set stones, to work in wood and to engage in all kinds of artistic crafts."** This passage shows that God is the source of all creative arts, inspiration, and craftsmanship and puts those artistic skills and talents within us. When we lean into our creative pursuits, we are leaning into the talents and gifts God has uniquely given us. He delights in seeing us use those talents for His glory and to bring ourselves and others joy.

Psalm 33:3 encourages us to **"Sing to him a new song; play skillfully, and shout for joy."** Music and art have always been powerful forms of worship, bringing communities together and lifting our spirits. When we create beautiful sounds, whether through playing an instrument or crafting a new musical piece, we can do it with joy, knowing that God rejoices with us. There's something beautiful in putting your heart into a song or project and feeling that it's not just your voice or hands working—it's God's Spirit moving through you.

Even practical expressions like gardening or sewing can carry deep spiritual meaning. **Exodus 35:35** tells us that God **"has filled them with skill to do all kinds of work as engravers, designers, embroiderers in blue, purple and scarlet yarn and fine linen, and weavers—all skilled workers and designers."** Every stitch, every plant placed in the soil, and every woven pattern can become an act of worship when we do it with love and intention. When I tend to a garden or create something tangible with my hands, I feel connected to the Creator who made it all. It's a reminder of His intricate design and care for even the most minor details.

I've also found that sharing my creative work, whether it's writing or something else, also becomes a way to touch the lives of others. Art and creativity speak to the soul in ways that words alone often cannot. When we create with the love and truth of God woven into it, the Holy Spirit can use it to touch hearts and draw people closer to Him. The beauty we create can be a beacon that points others to the source of all beauty—God Himself and be a way to bring honor to Him.

So, how can we incorporate more Christian creative expression into our daily lives?

1. **Make Time for Creativity:** Dedicate time each week for creative expression, whether drawing, writing, or working on a craft project. Don't wait for the perfect time; make time and show up with what you have.

2. **Invite God Into the Process:** Start your creative time with a simple prayer: "God, guide my hands and heart as I create. Let this be an offering to You." This sets the tone and reminds you that you're not creating alone.

3. **Create Without Fear:** Remember **Colossians 3:23**—work at it with all your heart, as for the Lord. Don't worry if your art or creation isn't perfect. God delights in your effort and your heart behind it.

4. **Share Your Work:** Don't be afraid to share what you create with others. Whether you show it to a friend or post it online, your work could inspire or comfort someone in ways you don't even realize.

5. **Celebrate Others' Creativity:** Encourage and support friends or family in their creative pursuits. Just as God delights in our creativity, we should find joy in seeing others express their gifts.

Christian creative expression isn't just about making something beautiful; it's about connecting with God, experiencing the joy of the Holy Spirit, and reflecting His glory in our unique way. Let's embrace our God-given creativity, knowing that we're worshiping the One who first created us in every brushstroke, note, stitch, or word.

Reflection and Discussion Questions:

As we meditate on this week's study verses: **Proverbs 8:30-31, Colossians 3:23, Psalm 33:3, Exodus 35:31-33,** and **Exodus 35:35, what common theme** is the Lord showing or revealing to you about joy?

_____

_____

What do you think the Lord Jesus **would like you to understand from these verses** about His joy and how it completely fills, strengthens, and transforms the lives of those who love and obey Him?

_____

_____

Application:

What are **two (2) practical ways** we can apply what we have studied to our lives this coming week? You can choose from the list of suggestions or list some of your own.

1._____

_____

2._____

_____

What good things do you expect to happen as we apply these truths to our lives?

1._____

_____

2._____

_____

Simple Prayer:

Dear Lord, we are so thankful for the gift of creativity that you have given us. Help us to find joy in expressing ourselves through art, music, writing, and other creative ways. May our creative pursuits bring glory to your name and be a source of inspiration and happiness for others. In Jesus' name, we pray. Amen.

Chapter Thirteen

Unquenchable Joy-Week 13

*"...so that you may live a life worthy of the Lord and please him in every way: bearing fruit in every good work, growing in the knowledge of God, being strengthened with all power according to his glorious might so that you may have great endurance and patience, **and giving Joyful thanks to the Father.**"*
Colossians 1:10-12

Study and Meditation for the Week: Joy in the Midst of Adversity

Daily practices like prayer, worship, and Bible study are the heartbeat of a joyful, purpose-filled life. They don't just help us achieve our goals and see our dreams come to pass—they also carry us through the darker, more challenging times we all inevitably face. I can share that during some of my hardest seasons, the closeness of the Lord gave me strength, and I've learned that joy isn't dependent on my circumstances because it's rooted in the Lord, not in what's happening around me and as I trusted in Him, He has transformed my darkest situations time and time again.

Psalm 30:11-12 beautifully captures this transformation: **"You turned my wailing into dancing; you removed my sackcloth and**

clothed me with joy, that my heart may sing your praises and not be silent. Lord my God, I will praise you forever." These verses remind me that even in the darkest moments, God is working to bring restoration and joy. It might not always happen as quickly as we'd like, but when we stay close to Him through prayer and worship, He lifts our spirits and fills us with His unshakable joy.

One of the other things I've learned is that joy isn't about denying our pain or pretending everything is fine. It's about finding hope and strength in the Lord, even when life feels heavy. **Isaiah 61:3** promises that God will give us **"a crown of beauty instead of ashes, the oil of joy instead of mourning, and a garment of praise instead of a spirit of despair."** This exchange is so powerful. When we bring our brokenness to God in prayer, He replaces it with something beautiful—joy that sustains us, even in the midst of hardship.

I remember a season when I felt utterly overwhelmed by the challenges in my life. It was hard to see past the weight of what I was facing in my family, but I made a commitment to spend time with God each morning. Some days, all I could do was sit quietly, whispering prayers for strength. Other days, I poured out my heart, telling God everything I was struggling with. Those moments became a refuge for me—a place where I could lay down my burdens and pick up His peace. **Psalm 63:5-8** reflects this so well: **"I will be fully satisfied as with the richest of foods; with singing lips, my mouth will praise you. On my bed I remember you; I think of you through the watches of the night. Because you are my help, I sing in the shadow of your wings. I cling to you; your right hand upholds me."**

The more I leaned into those daily prayer, worship, and Bible study practices, the more I felt my perspective shift. God's Word began to feel alive in my heart, reminding me of His promises and His faithfulness. **Colossians 1:10-12** became a guide for me during that time: "**...so that you may live a life worthy of the Lord and please him in every way: bearing fruit in every good work, growing in the knowledge of God, being strengthened with all power according to his glorious might so that you may have great endurance and patience, and giving joyful thanks to the Father.**" I found that as I pressed into Jesus, I began to experience the strength and endurance I needed to move forward, one day at a time.

One of the most beautiful truths I've discovered is that joy and pain can coexist, that even in our times of adversity, the Lord can provide times of joy. **Psalm 126:5-6** says, "**Those who sow with tears will reap with songs of joy. Those who go out weeping, carrying seed to sow, will return with songs of joy, carrying sheaves with them.**" This reminds me that even in seasons of sorrow, there is hope; we are never hopeless! God uses those seasons to plant seeds of growth and transformation that will eventually produce a harvest of joy. When we choose to keep seeking Him, even through our tears, we're sowing into something greater than we can ever imagine.

Romans 5:3-5 reinforces this perspective: "**Not only so, but we also glory in our sufferings, because we know that suffering produces perseverance; perseverance, character; and character, hope. And hope does not put us to shame, because God's love has been poured out into our hearts through the Holy Spirit, who has been given to us.**" These verses remind me that every trial we walk through has a purpose. God uses even our hardest moments to shape us, strengthen us, and draw us closer to Him. And through it all, His love remains constant, pouring into our hearts and filling us with hope.

So, how can we make these daily practices a consistent part of our lives, even when things feel overwhelming? Here are a few things that have helped me:

1. Start Small and Stay Consistent

If you're feeling stuck or overwhelmed, begin with just five minutes of prayer or Bible reading each day. Consistency is more important than quantity. Over time, you'll naturally want to spend more time with God as you experience the peace and joy He brings.

2. Create a Worshipful Environment

Find ways to make worship a regular part of your day, whether it's through music, journaling, or simply sitting in silence. **Isaiah 61:3** reminds us that praise can lift our spirits, replacing despair with joy. Even turning on a worship playlist while you cook or drive can transform your mindset.

3. Meditate on Scripture

Choose a verse that speaks to your current season, like **Psalm 30:11-12** or **Romans 5:3-5**, and reflect on it throughout the day. Write it on a sticky note or save it as your phone background to keep it in front of you.

4. Keep a Gratitude Journal

Writing down even three things you're thankful for each day can shift your perspective and help you see God's hand in your life. **Psalm 126:5-6** reminds us that joy often comes after seasons of sowing, so celebrate the small victories and blessings along the way.

5. Lean on Community

Sometimes, joy feels hard to find on our own. Surround yourself with people who will pray for you, encourage you, and remind you of God's promises. Share your struggles and victories with others—it's a beautiful way to experience His love through community.

6. Make Prayer a Conversation

Prayer doesn't have to be formal or complicated. Talk to God throughout your day, sharing your thoughts, fears, and joys with Him. **Psalm 63:5-8** shows us that God's presence is a place of refuge and joy, so let prayer be your way of staying connected to Him.

Daily practices like prayer, worship, and Bible study aren't just about checking off a list—they're about drawing closer to the One who sustains us. In every season, whether joyful or challenging, these habits anchor us in His love and give us the strength and perspective we need to keep moving forward. Let's choose to embrace these practices, trusting that God will meet us in them and fill our hearts with unquenchable joy.

Reflection and Discussion Questions:

As we meditate on this week's study verses: **Colossians 1:10-12, Psalm 30:11-12, Isaiah 61:3, Psalm 63:5-8, Psalm 126:5-6,** and **Romans 5:3-5, what common theme** is the Lord showing or revealing to you about joy?

_____

_____

What do you think the Lord Jesus would like you to understand from these verses about His joy and how it completely fills, strengthens, and transforms the lives of those who love and obey Him?

_____

_____

Application:

What are **two (2) practical ways** we can apply what we have studied to our lives this coming week? You can choose from the list of suggestions or list some of your own.

1._____

_____

2._____

_____

What good things do you expect to happen as we apply these truths to our lives?

1._____

_____

2._____

_____

Simple Prayer:

Father, thank you for always being close when I am going through hard times. Knowing you are near, that you hold me and care for me more than I care for my own loved ones, strengthens me and gives me comfort. I love you. In Jesus' name, we pray. Amen.

Chapter Fourteen

Unquenchable Joy-Week 14

*"Will You not revive us again, that Your people **may rejoice in You?"** Psalm 85:6*

Study and Meditation for the Week: Strength for the Journey

*The following is an excerpt from my chapter "Refresh, Renew, Refill for the Journey," published in: *Unstoppable Woman: The Journey Continues*

Renewal is defined as making new; every child in my special education classroom always knew it was a new day when they stepped into my classroom each morning. It did not matter what the day before had been like, what chairs might have been tossed, what rash and heated words might have been spoken, or what other negative things might have happened. It was a brand new, shiny, clean slate of a day. Renewed, and we were going to have the best day ever!

We can all benefit from that mindset; if all of yesterday's failures were gone, how would you approach today? If every negative thought you had, everything from the day before, was absent, and you only had good things in front of you, no nagging voices from your past, what could stop you from succeeding today? If you woke up each day telling yourself, "This will be my best day ever!" what could stop you or be beyond you? This positive self-reflection empowers us to learn, heal from past mistakes, and move forward with a renewed sense of purpose and freedom.

Embracing this process allows us to examine and renew our thoughts, attitudes, and behaviors, fostering positive change in our lives. Renewal often provides a profound sense of purpose, meaning, and hope. This hope bolsters our resilience, empowers us to navigate life's challenges with unwavering optimism, and fosters a renewed sense of fulfillment and joy.

I had a distinct advantage in my life to be the person to tell a classroom of students who had not experienced a great deal of success in their lives that message every day because I had to believe it myself. "Can't" was a word that was not allowed in my classroom. We replaced it with "Yet." If a student said, "I can't do that," the response was, "You can't do that YET." What have you not done Yet? What dream do you have that needs to be made new again? What skill you planned on learning have you yet to learn?

I am notorious for going from one creative medium to another. My current obsession is fabric coloring with special ink pencils that look like regular watercolor pencils drawings until they are activated with a medium that makes the color suddenly become vivid, bright, and permanent on the fabric. The change is a fantastic transformation, and I am always fascinated by it. The soft colors are beautiful on their own, with subtle shading and soft colors, but when they are activated, and the ink within becomes visible, the full spectrum of their true beauty within is revealed. In that same way, our hidden tablets, strengths, and needs to be revealed through ongoing self-renewal.

This self-renewal is essential for maintaining physical, emotional, and spiritual well-being in a world marked by constant challenges and adversities. We all need that activation, that newness that reveals the extra hidden beauty within us. The new thing no one ever saw, but was there all the time waiting for the right time, the right situation or circumstance to bring about that activation.

The constant renewing through my faith offers a transformative journey that encompasses forgiveness, personal transformation, strength in adversity, purpose, and hope. Drawing from Christ's teachings and the Bible's timeless wisdom, I find the inspiration and guidance to navigate life's complexities and emerge more substantial and renewed. My faith's emphasis on forgiveness, personal growth, resilience, purpose, and eternal hope makes it a powerful catalyst for positive change and self-renewal in an ever-changing world. May today and tomorrow be the days you are renewed and activated through faith that you have what you need to succeed, honest self-reflection on where you are, and letting go of any past failures holding you back from your best days ever!

Reflection and Discussion Questions:

As we meditate on this week's passage and **Psalm 85:6,** our chapter-opening verse, what is the Lord **showing or revealing to you about the connection between renewal and joy?**

_____

_____

What do you think the Lord Jesus **would like you to understand** from this week's study about His joy and how it strengthens and transforms the lives of those who love and obey Him?

_____

_____

Application:

What are **two (2) practical ways** we can apply what we have looked at in this chapter to our lives this coming week?

1._____

_____

2._____

_____

What good things do you expect to happen as we apply these truths to our lives?

1._____

_____

2._____

_____

Simple Prayer:

Lord, thank you for constantly renewing me. Show me the hidden things you have placed in me, so I can use them to further the Kingdom, help others, and grow in my love of you. In Jesus' name, I pray. Amen.

Chapter Fifteen

Unquenchable Joy-Week 15

"There is a time for everything and a season for every activity under the heavens." **Ecclesiastes 3:1**

Study and Meditation for the Week: Season of Waiting

Life is a journey of seasons, each bringing its own unique challenges and blessings. Some seasons are filled with momentum and progress, while others feel like everything is on pause. I've walked through both, and I've learned this: Embracing each season with a heart full of joy helps us navigate it with grace and strength. It's not always easy, but when we trust that God is working in and through every season, we can find joy and peace even in the midst of uncertainty. **Ecclesiastes 3:1** reminds us, **"There is a time for everything and a season for every activity under the heavens."** This truth anchors me when life feels unpredictable.

Seasons change—sometimes quickly, sometimes slowly—but God is constant. Whether we're experiencing a season of abundance or a season of waiting, He's always there, guiding us through it. Recognizing this builds our relationship with Him and helps us find joy in the midst of whatever season we're in. One of the hardest seasons to endure is the season of waiting. Waiting for a breakthrough, a job, a relationship, or an answer to prayer can feel like an eternity. I've been there—praying, hoping, and wondering if God heard me. **Psalm 27:14** encourages us, **"Wait for the Lord; be strong and take heart and wait for the Lord."** Waiting requires trust, and trust is built when we remember that God's timing is perfect. Even when we can't see it, He's working behind the scenes, aligning everything according to His plan.

Psalm 33:20-22 has also been a lifeline for me in these moments: **"We wait in hope for the Lord; he is our help and our shield. In him, our hearts rejoice, for we trust in his holy name. May your unfailing love be with us, Lord, even as we put our hope in you."** Waiting isn't passive; it's an active posture of hope and trust in God. When we fix our eyes on Him, we find joy even in waiting because we know He is faithful.

Lamentations 3:22-26 is another reminder of God's faithfulness during uncertain seasons: **"Because of the Lord's great love we are not consumed, for his compassions never fail. They are new every morning; great is your faithfulness. I say to myself, 'The Lord is my portion; therefore, I will wait for him.' The Lord is good to those whose hope is in him, to the one who seeks him; it is good to wait quietly for the salvation of the Lord."** God's mercies are new every morning, and His love sustains us as we wait. Even in the waiting, we can experience His goodness.

During a particularly long season of waiting in my life, I started praying **Psalm 5:3** each morning: **"In the morning, Lord, you hear my voice; in the morning, I lay my requests before you and wait expectantly."** That word—expectantly—shifted my perspective. Instead of focusing on what hadn't happened yet, I started to look for signs of God's hand in my life each day. And you know what? They were always there. Sometimes, it was a kind word from a friend, a moment of peace in prayer, or a verse that spoke directly to my heart. Those small reminders of His presence gave me the strength to keep going.

Psalm 40:1-3 beautifully captures the transformation that happens when we trust God through the waiting: **"I waited patiently for the Lord; he turned to me and heard my cry. He lifted me out of the slimy pit, out of the mud and mire; he set my feet on a rock and gave me a firm place to stand. He put a new song in my mouth, a hymn of praise to our God."** God doesn't just leave us in the waiting—He rescues, restores, and gives us a new song. That new song is the joy that comes from seeing His faithfulness unfold.

Isaiah 25:9 encourages us to hold on to that joy: **"In that day they will say, 'Surely this is our God; we trusted in him, and he saved us. This is the Lord, we trusted in him; let us rejoice and be glad in his salvation."** When we finally see the fruit of the season we've walked through, we can rejoice in knowing that God was with us every step of the way, even when it was hard to see.

Here are some ways we can embrace joy and trust God in every season:

1. **Start Your Day in Prayer:** As **Psalm 5:3** suggests, lay your requests before God in the morning and wait expectantly. Let prayer be the way you align your heart with His plans for the day.

2. **Look for Small Blessings:** Even in seasons of waiting, God's goodness is all around us. Keep a gratitude journal or take a moment each day to thank Him for the little things that bring joy and peace.

3. **Meditate on God's Promises:** Spend time in the Word, focusing on verses like **Lamentations 3:22-26** and **Psalm 33:20-22**. Let these truths remind you that God is faithful and His love never fails.

4. **Share Your Journey:** Talk to someone you trust about the season you're in. Their perspective and encouragement can help you see God's hand in ways you might have missed.

5. **Worship While You Wait:** Worship shifts our focus from our circumstances to God's greatness. Whether it's through music, journaling, or quiet reflection, take time to praise Him for who He is.

We need to always remember that while life's seasons come and go, God remains constant. Whether we're waiting, rejoicing, or walking through challenges, we can find joy and strength in Him. Let's embrace every season with faith, knowing God is always working for our good and His glory.

Reflection and Discussion Questions:

As we meditate on this week's study verses: **Ecclesiastes 3:1, Psalm 27:14, Psalm 33:20-22, Lamentations 3:22-26, Psalm 5:3,** and **Psalm 40:1-3, and Isaiah 25:9, what common theme** is the Lord showing or revealing to you about joy?

_____

_____

What do you think the Lord Jesus **would like you to understand from these verses** about His joy and how it completely fills, strengthens, and transforms the lives of those who love and obey Him?

_____

_____

Application:

What are **two (2) practical ways** we can apply what we have studied to our lives this coming week? You can choose from the list of suggestions or list some of your own.

1._____

_____

2._____

_____

What good things do you expect to happen as we apply these truths to our lives?

1._____

_____

2._____

_____

Simple Prayer:

Lord, thank you for being with me in all the seasons of my life. Fill me with the joy that faith and confidence in you bring. Teach me to recognize your nearness and faithfulness as I wait expectantly for you to move in my season of waiting. In Jesus' name, we pray. Amen.

Chapter Sixteen

Unquenchable Joy-Week 16

"That person is like a tree planted by streams of water,
which yields its fruit in season and whose leaf does not
wither —whatever they do prospers."
Psalm 1:1-3

Study and Meditation for the Week:
Season of Growth

I live in a fruitful agricultural area of Northern California. Orchards surround me, and the many fields are full of various crops yearly. We count the seasons in the fruit and olive orchards, winery vineyards, rice fields, and the acres of nut trees that dot our landscape. Our farmer's markets brim with local produce that testifies to the rich, fertile land we live in. Our spring seasons are beautiful, with the colorful blossoming of the fruit trees and new growth in the fields.

Living in Northern California, surrounded by these orchards, vineyards, and fields, has given me a deep appreciation for the rhythm of growth and transformation in nature. In the spring, the vibrant blossoms on the fruit trees and the green carpets stretching across the foothills are breathtaking reminders of new beginnings and potential. Driving through the countryside during this season feels like driving through a picture of hope and renewal. But the beauty we see in those blossoms doesn't come without hard work—there's a process to growth. This process of growth often involves stretching in ways that feel uncomfortable, breaking through what holds you back, and facing challenges that can feel overwhelming but are essential for transformation.

I've realized that seasons of growth in our lives mirror what I see in those orchards and fields. Growth often comes with discomfort, even resistance, as we're stretched and called to leave the familiar behind. Seeds have to push against the soil to break through to the sunlight, and in the same way, we have to move past our comfort zones to step into what God has planned for us. It's not easy, but it's necessary and worth it.

James 1:4 reminds us, **"Let perseverance finish its work so that you may be mature and complete, not lacking anything."** Growth is about perseverance, allowing God to work in and through us during those harsh seasons. It's about trusting that He's making us mature and complete, shaping us into people ready for the next step in His plan. When I face those seasons of stretching, I often feel like resisting, like clinging to what's comfortable and safe. But I've learned that the real joy comes when I lean into the process and trust that God is at work, even when it's hard to see.

2 Corinthians 3:18 says, **"And we all, who with unveiled faces contemplate the Lord's glory, are being transformed into his image with ever-increasing glory, which comes from the Lord, who is the Spirit."** Growth is about transformation, becoming more like Christ. Transformation isn't a one-time event; it's a continuous process of being molded and shaped by God. It's not always easy, but when I remind myself that He's transforming me into His image, I find peace in the process.

Ephesians 4:22-24 puts it this way: "**You were taught, with regard to your former way of life, to put off your old self...to be made new in the attitude of your minds; and to put on the new self, created to be like God in true righteousness and holiness.**" Growth involves shedding the old, letting go of habits, thoughts, or fears that no longer serve us, and stepping into the new self that God is calling us to be. It's a process of renewal that requires trust and a willingness to change, even when it's uncomfortable.

I often think about the trees and crops around me. They don't just grow; they are nourished. They draw water from the soil, soak up sunlight, and receive care from the farmers who tend them. Similarly, our growth depends on staying connected to our source—God. **Psalm 1:1-3** describes this beautifully: "**That person is like a tree planted by streams of water, which yields its fruit in season and whose leaf does not wither—whatever they do prospers.**" When we stay rooted in God's Word and presence, we're nourished and able to grow, even during seasons of drought or difficulty.

Isaiah 58:11 promises us that God will guide us through these seasons of growth: "**The Lord will guide you always; he will satisfy your needs in a sun-scorched land and will strengthen your frame. You will be like a well-watered garden, like a spring whose waters never fail.**" This verse reminds me that even in the most challenging seasons, God provides the strength and nourishment we need to thrive. He doesn't leave us to struggle alone; He is always there, guiding and sustaining us.

Growth isn't just about what God is doing in us—it's also about how He equips us to help others grow. As we are stretched and transformed, we become better able to encourage and support others in their journeys. **2 Corinthians 5:17** says, "**Therefore, if anyone is in Christ, the new creation has come: The old has gone, the new is**

here!" Our transformation isn't just for us; it's a testimony to the power of God's work in our lives and an invitation for others to experience that same renewal.

So, how can we embrace these seasons of growth with joy and trust?

1. **Stay Rooted in God's Word:** Like the tree planted by streams of water in **Psalm 1:1-3**, stay connected to God through prayer, Bible study, and worship. Let His Word nourish you and give you strength for the journey.

2. **Trust the Process:** Remember **James 1:4** and let perseverance finish its work. Growth takes time, and it's okay not to see immediate results. Trust that God is working, even when it feels slow or challenging.

3. **Celebrate Small Steps:** Growth doesn't always come in big, apparent leaps. Sometimes, it's the small steps forward that matter most. Celebrate those moments and thank God for His faithfulness.

4. **Lean on Community:** Just as orchards thrive when they are part of a larger ecosystem, we grow best when surrounded by others who encourage and support us. Share your journey with trusted friends or mentors.

5. **Look for the Fruit:** Even in seasons of stretching, look for signs of God's work in your life. Whether it's a new perspective, a moment of peace, or an opportunity to help someone else, these are glimpses of the fruit He's growing in you.

Seasons of growth may not always be easy, but they are where God does some of His most beautiful work. Let's embrace them, trusting that He is transforming, equipping, and preparing us for the amazing things He has planned.

Reflection and Discussion Questions:

As we meditate on this week's study verses: **James 1:4, 2 Corinthians 3:18, Ephesians 4:22-24, Psalm 1:1-3, Isaiah 58:11,** and **2 Corinthians 5:17, what common theme** is the Lord showing or revealing to you about joy?

_____

_____

What do you think the Lord Jesus **would like you to understand from these verses** about His joy and how it completely fills, strengthens, and transforms the lives of those who love and obey Him?

_____

_____

Application:

What are **two (2) practical ways** we can apply what we have studied to our lives this coming week? You can choose from the list of suggestions or list some of your own.

1._____

_____

2._____

_____

What good things do you expect to happen as we apply these truths to our lives?

1._____

_____

2._____

_____

Simple Prayer:

Lord, thank you for helping me grow daily into your vision of me. You and you alone give me my identity and say who I am. Help me to joyfully go through the process of my growth and transformation hand in hand with you. In Jesus' name, we pray. Amen.

Chapter Seventeen

Unquenchable Joy-Week 17

"For seven days, celebrate the festival to the Lord your God at the place the Lord will choose. For the Lord your God will bless you in all your harvest and in all the work of your hands, and your joy will be complete."
Deuteronomy 16:15

Study and Meditation for the Week:
Season of Harvest

My dad JW was the harvest boss for decades for one of the largest agricultural ranches in the San Joaquin Valley in Central California. He maintained and ran all the harvesting equipment and worker crews. Each year, massive truckloads of cantaloupe, tomatoes, and other crops were planted, grown, and harvested for the local packing sheds. The hundreds of acres of fields were carefully managed with crops that were rotated, so there was very little time in the year that one field section or another was not in the process of either getting ready for planting, growing a crop, or being harvested.

In the summer, when most of the valley tomatoes were harvested, the huge harvesting equipment ran around the clock. The sight of those huge harvesters moving across the fields at night under the giant field lights, each one with a crew of workers standing on them working the conveyor assembly line, demonstrated the importance of the harvest in due time. Harvest time waits for no one, and is the culmination of months of planning and care.

Seasons of life can be as varied and distinct as the ones we see in nature. Living in rhythm with these seasons—both the blessings and the challenges—teaches us to lean into God's timing and purposes. I often think about how each season has its unique beauty and its specific work, whether it's a season of sowing, growth, harvest, or rest. Learning to embrace each one has been a journey for me, but it's a journey that has deepened my faith and brought me closer to God.

Hosea 10:12 says, **"Sow righteousness for yourselves, reap the fruit of unfailing love, and break up your unplowed ground; for it is time to seek the Lord, until he comes and showers his righteousness on you."** This verse reminds me that every season has its work, and often that work requires preparation. Just like farmers have to break up the hard ground before they can plant seeds, we sometimes need to let God break up the hardened places in our hearts. That process can be uncomfortable, but it's necessary for growth and for the joy that comes from seeing God's love and righteousness take root in our lives.

I've had seasons where I felt like I was doing nothing but sowing—working hard, praying, and trusting without seeing much fruit. Those times can feel discouraging, but **Jeremiah 5:24** reminds us of God's faithfulness: **"They do not say to themselves, 'Let us fear the Lord our God, who gives autumn and spring rains in season, who assures us of the regular weeks of harvest.'"** God is the one who brings the rain and the harvest, in His perfect timing. That's a truth I hold onto when I'm in a season of waiting, knowing that the work I'm doing now—whether it's in my spiritual life, my relationships, or my goals—will bear fruit in its time.

Ecclesiastes 3:1-2 speaks to this rhythm of life: "**There is a time for everything, and a season for every activity under the heavens: a time to be born and a time to die, a time to plant and a time to uproot.**" When I'm in a season of planting, I often want to skip ahead to the harvest. But planting is essential—it's the foundation for what's to come. It's during these seasons that I've learned to trust God's timing and embrace the process, knowing that He's at work even when I can't yet see the results.

One of the most beautiful seasons is the season of harvest, when we get to see the fruit of what's been planted and tended. **Deuteronomy 16:15** captures the joy of harvest so well: "**For the Lord your God will bless you in all your harvest and in all the work of your hands, and your joy will be complete.**" Those moments of harvest, when we see the tangible results of God's blessings, are opportunities to celebrate and give thanks. But even in the joy of harvest, I've learned to stay humble and remember that the work doesn't end there. God often uses those seasons to prepare us for the next step in His plan.

In **Luke 10:2,** Jesus tells His disciples, "**The harvest is plentiful, but the workers are few. Ask the Lord of the harvest, therefore, to send out workers into his harvest field.**" This verse reminds me that harvest isn't just about personal blessings—it's also about being part of God's work in the world. When we've been through seasons of growth and harvest, we're equipped to help others. Whether it's sharing the gospel, encouraging a friend, or serving our community, we're called to be workers in God's field, helping others experience the same joy and transformation that He's brought to us.

So, how can we embrace the different seasons of life with faith, joy, and purpose? Here are a few lessons I've learned along the way:

1. **Recognize the Season You're In:** Take time to reflect on where you are right now. Are you in a season of planting, where you're working and praying without yet seeing results? Or are you in a season of harvest, where you're enjoying the blessings of what God has done? Identifying your season helps you align your expectations and focus on what God is teaching you in this moment.

2. **Be Patient in the Planting:** Planting and waiting go hand in hand. Whether you're building a relationship, working toward a goal, or growing in your faith, it takes time for seeds to sprout and grow. Trust that God is working beneath the surface, even when you can't see it yet. **Hosea 10:12** reminds us to seek the Lord while we're sowing, trusting Him to bring the rain and the harvest.

3. **Celebrate the Small Wins:** In every season, there are moments to celebrate. Maybe it's a small breakthrough in a relationship, an answered prayer, or just the strength to take another step forward. **Deuteronomy 16:15** reminds us that joy comes from recognizing and celebrating God's blessings, big or small.

4. **Stay Rooted in God's Word:** Like a tree planted by streams of water, staying rooted in God's Word helps us thrive in every season. Spend time daily in prayer and Bible study, letting God nourish your spirit and guide your steps. This keeps you grounded and gives you the strength to face both the challenges and the joys of each season.

5. **Be Willing to Uproot When Necessary: Ecclesiastes 3:2** talks about a time to plant and a time to uproot. Sometimes, growth means letting go—of habits, relationships, or plans

that no longer align with God's will. Trust that when God calls you to uproot something, it's because He's making room for something better.

6. **Prepare for the Harvest:** When the season of harvest comes, it can be overwhelming. The blessings may be abundant, but so is the work. **Luke 10:2** reminds us that we're called to be workers in God's field, helping to gather the harvest and share His love with others. Be ready to step into those opportunities with joy and gratitude.

7. **Trust the Process:** Every season serves a purpose. Whether it's breaking up hard ground, planting seeds, waiting for rain, or reaping the harvest, God is in every part of the process. **Jeremiah 5:24** reminds us of His faithfulness to provide in every season. Trust that He's working all things together for good, even when the path isn't clear.

As we walk through the seasons of life, let's remember that God is with us in each one. He's the Lord of the harvest, the one who brings the rain, and the one who turns our sowing into reaping. Whether we're planting in faith or celebrating the fruit of our labor, we can find joy in knowing that He is at work, shaping us, blessing us, and using us for His glory. Let's embrace each season with open hearts, trusting that His timing and His plans are always perfect.

Reflection and Discussion Questions:

As we meditate on this week's study verses: **Deuteronomy 16:15, Hosea 10:12, Jeremiah 5:24, Ecclesiastes 3:1-2,** and **Luke 10:2, what common theme** is the Lord showing or revealing to you about joy?

_____

_____

What do you think the Lord Jesus **would like you to understand from these verses** about His joy and how it completely fills, strengthens, and transforms the lives of those who love and obey Him?

_____

_____

Application:

What are **two (2) practical ways** we can apply what we have studied to our lives this coming week?

1._____

_____

2._____

_____

What good things do you expect to happen as we apply these truths to our lives?

1._____

_____

2._____

_____

Simple Prayer:

Lord Jesus, thank you for giving us seasons and showing us your perfect timing in them. Let me see how I can help you in your work, gathering in the bountiful harvest you have for me and the Kingdom of God. In Jesus' name, I pray. Amen.

Chapter Eighteen

Unquenchable Joy-Week 18

"Though you have not seen Him, you love Him;
and even though you do not see him now, you believe
*and are **filled with an inexpressible and glorious joy.**"*
1 Peter 1:8

Meditation and Bible Study Review Weeks 1-4

Week 1- Weekly Bible Study Review: Discovering Unquenchable Joy

This week's Bible study focused on the concept of joy—specifically, the unshakable, lasting joy that comes from a deep relationship with Jesus Christ. We reflected on how easy it is to tie our sense of happiness to accomplishments or the expectations of others, which can lead to feelings of disappointment in ourselves. It was reassuring to know this is a common struggle, but the study pointed to a greater truth: true joy doesn't depend on circumstances but on God.

The study highlighted key scriptures that emphasize this deeper joy found in a relationship with God. **John 15:11** stood out: **"I have told you this so that my joy may be in you and that your joy may be complete."** This verse offers a reminder that Jesus provides a joy that is whole and fulfilling. **Nehemiah 8:10** added another layer, declaring, **"The joy of the Lord is your strength,"** encouraging us to view joy as a source of resilience and energy in the face of challenges.

The study also focused on aligning our lives with God's biblical principles, not as burdensome rules, but as pathways for us to discover true joy. These principles were presented as tools for building a strong and steady foundation that sustains and empowers believers through life's highs and lows.

These scriptures inspired and equipped us to seek joy more intentionally, finding strength in God's presence and promises, and offered hope, encouragement, and practical steps for cultivating lasting joy rooted in faith.

Week 2- Devotion Review:
Cultivating a Joyful and Grateful Heart

This week's devotion centered on the beautiful connection between joy and gratitude, showing how one naturally feeds into the other when we step into God's presence. The message was clear: Cultivating a heart of gratitude isn't just a nice idea; it's a biblical principle that transforms our perspective and fills us with unshakable joy.

We studied **1 Thessalonians 5:16-18**, where Paul calls us to **"rejoice always, pray continually, give thanks in all circumstances."** This verse reminded us that gratitude and joy are choices we make daily, not based on how we feel or what we face, but on God's goodness and faithfulness. **Ezra 3:11** and **1 Chronicles 16:34** illustrated this beautifully, with examples of people praising God in the middle of their struggles because they trusted His enduring love.

The practical steps for cultivating gratitude were especially inspiring. Starting each day by listing three things to be thankful for felt like an achievable way to set a positive tone. Keeping a gratitude journal and speaking thankfulness out loud were other simple yet powerful habits. Even in hard times, we were encouraged to thank God for His presence, which shifts our focus from our problems to His faithfulness.

Reflecting on God's goodness, both past and present, was a recurring theme. It reminded us that gratitude isn't about pretending everything is perfect—it's about trusting that God is with us, working all things for good. This week's devotion left us with practical tools and a renewed sense of hope, encouraging us to look for His blessings daily and let joy and gratitude shape our lives.

Week 3- Devotion Review:
Faith—The Foundation of Unquenchable Joy

This week's devotion focused on the profound connection between faith and joy, emphasizing how faith serves as the unshakable foundation for a joyful life. Drawing from **Hebrews 11:1**, which defines faith as **"confidence in what we hope for and assurance about what we do not see,"** we explored how trusting in God's promises brings deep, abiding joy, even when the outcomes are not yet visible.

Psalm 16:11 reminded us of the joy found in God's presence: **"You make known to me the path of life; you will fill me with joy in your presence."** This assurance of God's nearness helps us navigate life's ups and downs with confidence and joy. **Jeremiah 29:11** further strengthened this truth, reassuring us that God's plans for us are good, filled with hope and a future.

The devotion encouraged us to build "remembrance altars" in our hearts—moments where we recall God's past faithfulness in our lives. Like the people in the Bible who created markers to remember God's provision, we, too, can grow our faith by reflecting on how He has carried us through challenges.

Philippians 1:25 reminded us that joy and faith grow together. As our faith deepens, we experience more joy, even in adversity, knowing God's promises are sure. This week's study was a powerful reminder to let faith guide us into unshakable joy, rooted in God's unchanging love and His faithfulness to fulfill His plans for our lives.

Week 4- Devotion Review:
Trust—The Anchor of Joy and Peace

This week's devotion focused on the transformative power of trusting God's sovereignty and goodness. Trust, we learned, is more than a feeling—it's an intentional act of releasing our fears and relying on God's wisdom and faithfulness. **Proverbs 3:5-6** reminded us to trust in the Lord with all our hearts, lean not on our own understanding, and submit to Him in all things, knowing He will make our paths straight.

The connection between trust and joy was a central theme. **Psalm 28:7** highlighted that trusting God doesn't just bring peace but also strength and joy. When we rely on Him, we're reminded that we're never alone in life's uncertainties. Trust, as **Psalm 52:8** portrays, allows us to flourish like olive trees—steadfast and thriving, rooted in God's unfailing love, even during life's storms.

Practical steps helped bring trust into daily life. Starting the day by acknowledging God's control, turning worries into prayers, and speaking trust out loud were simple yet impactful practices to incorporate this week. Leaning on scriptures like **Psalm 91:2** as affirmations reinforced that trust isn't passive—it's active and life-changing.

This week's study left us with a deeper understanding of trust as an anchor that steadies us in life's chaos, replacing fear with peace and filling our hearts with unquenchable joy. By trusting in God, we can move forward with confidence, knowing He holds us securely in His love.

Reflection and Discussion Questions:

As you meditated on this four-week Bible study review, what new did you see, or what important thing were you reminded of?

_____

_____

How did this week's review deepen your understanding of the Lord?

_____

_____

Application:

What are **two (2) new ways** we can apply what we have studied this week to our lives?

1._____

_____

2._____

_____

Simple Prayer:

Lord, please cause me to rejoice always in you. Help me to remember that if everything in the world were wrong, it would not equal the righteousness and joy that exists because you exist. Help us to focus on you and the joy that you are by your very being. In Jesus' name, we pray. Amen.

Chapter Nineteen

Unquenchable Joy-Week 19

*"That which we have seen and heard we declare to you,
that you also may have fellowship with us; and truly
our fellowship is with the Father and with His Son Jesus
Christ. And these things write we unto you, that your
joy may be full." 1 John 1:3-4*

Study and Meditation for the Week:
Review of Weeks 5-8

Week 5- Bible Study Review:
Obedience—The Path to Lasting Joy

This week's Bible study shed new light on obedience, reframing it not as restrictive or burdensome but as a pathway to true and lasting joy. In **John 15:10-11**, Jesus reminds us that keeping His commandments allows us to remain in His love and experience a joy that is complete— whole and unshaken. The study emphasized that obedience is less about rules and more about walking in step with God's good and perfect plans for our lives.

Psalm 119:111 describes God's statutes as a "heritage forever" and "the joy of my heart," showing how obedience leads to a deep sense of fulfillment. **Psalm 19:8** further highlights how God's precepts bring clarity and light to our lives, helping us feel grounded and confident even when the road is challenging. Obedience, as the study revealed, aligns us with God's truth, filling our hearts with a resilient joy that isn't dependent on circumstances.

We were also encouraged to see joy in trials, as **James 1:2-3** teaches that hardships build perseverance and strengthen faith. Even in tough seasons, obedience draws us closer to God and fosters joy, not despair.

Week 6- Bible Study Review:
Joy in God's Presence

This week's Bible study reminded us of the incredible power of God's presence as our refuge in life's chaos. In those moments when everything feels overwhelming, and we're running on empty, turning to God brings peace and joy that nothing else can offer. **Psalm 16:11** beautifully describes it: **"In your presence, there is fullness of joy."** It's not just fleeting happiness but a deep, soul-filling joy that refreshes and sustains us.

The study emphasized that this joy isn't a one-time experience but a continual source of renewal. **Psalm 21:6** highlights how God grants us "unending blessings" and fills us with the joy of His presence, even when life throws us curveballs. Through examples like Job's restoration in **Job 33:26** and the early followers of Jesus in **Acts 2:28,** we were reminded that God's presence remains unchanging, even in the hardest times.

Practical steps helped bring these truths to life. Finding quiet moments to sit with God, bringing worship into everyday routines, praying throughout the day, and staying rooted in scripture were simple but powerful ways to stay connected to His presence. Verses like **Psalm 89:15-16** encouraged us to walk in God's light, celebrating His goodness and experiencing the joy that overflows into every part of our lives.

This Bible study left us inspired to seek God's presence more intentionally, knowing it's where true joy begins. No matter what we face, we can rest in the confidence that He is with us, filling us with strength, peace, and a joy that never fades.

Week 7- Bible Study Review:
The Joy of Community

This week's Bible study reminded us of the essential role a loving, faith-filled church community plays in our spiritual journey. Life wasn't meant to be lived alone; God designed us for fellowship, to share our joys and burdens with others. **Galatians 6:2** captures this beautifully: **"Carry each other's**

burdens, and in this way, you will fulfill the law of Christ." The strength and joy that come from walking through life together are irreplaceable.

The study highlighted how gathering with fellow believers creates a unique joy, as described in **Psalm 122:1: "I rejoiced with those who said to me, 'Let us go to the house of the Lord.'"** Whether worshiping, sharing testimonies, or simply spending time together, the connection we experience within a faith community strengthens our spirits and reminds us we're part of something greater. **Acts 2:46-47** painted a vivid picture of the early church—sharing meals, praising God, and celebrating life together, all with glad and sincere hearts.

Practical steps for fostering this kind of community included showing up regularly, being open and vulnerable, and celebrating both the highs and lows of life together. Encouraging one another and serving side by side were emphasized as powerful ways to deepen bonds and reflect God's love.

This Bible study left us inspired to lean into our church communities, not just for support but to experience the shared joy of walking with others in faith. It's in this fellowship that we grow stronger, feel God's love more tangibly, and live out His purpose together.

Week 8- Bible Study Review:
Daily Devotions—A Lifeline to Joy and Peace

This week's Bible study review reminded us that daily time with God isn't just another item on a to-do list—it's a lifeline. Spending time in prayer and God's Word is essential for deepening our relationship with Him and finding the peace, joy, and purpose we need to face life's challenges. **Psalm 143:8** beautifully sets the tone: **"Let the morning bring me word of your unfailing love, for I have put my trust in you."**

The study highlighted that daily devotion doesn't have to be perfect or elaborate; it's about showing up consistently and making space to meet with God. Whether in the quiet of the morning, during a midday break, or in reflective evening prayers, the key is prioritizing time with Him. Jesus Himself modeled this in **Mark 1:35**, retreating to pray in the early morning.

Practical tips like creating a sacred space, starting small with simple scripture readings and prayers, and remaining flexible on busy days made the practice feel accessible and sustainable. **Psalm 92:1-2** reminded us of the value of praising God both morning and night, using these moments to reflect, reset, and grow closer to Him.

This Bible Study emphasized that daily time with God isn't about perfection but connection. Each moment spent with Him fills us with His peace, roots us in His promises, and equips us to navigate life with joy, strength, and clarity. No matter how busy the day gets, it's a practice worth prioritizing.

Reflection and Discussion Questions:

As you meditated on this week's Bible study review: **What did** the Lord remind you of or reveal anew to you about joy?

_____

_____

Application:

How can we apply what we have studied this week to our lives?

_____

_____

Simple Prayer:

Lord, thank you for your word and the wisdom it contains. Show us the fullness of your joy when we stay connected to you and your word; continue to show us the work you have done in us and will continue to do so that our joy may be complete in you. In Jesus' name, we pray. Amen.

Chapter Twenty

Unquenchable Joy-Week 20

"I have told you this so that my joy may be in you and that your joy may be complete." **John 15:11**

Study and Meditation for the Week:
Review Weeks 9-12

Week 9- Bible Study Review:
Worship—A Transforming Act of Joy

This week's Bible study reframed worship as more than a Sunday activity; it's a way of life that shifts our hearts into alignment with God. Worship is our response to His greatness, a declaration of His unmatched power, and an acknowledgment of His unfailing love. **Psalm 9:2** captures it well: **"I will be glad and rejoice in you; I will sing the praises of your name, O Most High."** Worship fills us with joy that overflows into every area of life, lifting our spirits and renewing our perspective, even in challenging times.

We explored how worship isn't limited to singing or outward expressions. Sometimes, it's found in quiet moments of gratitude, like those described in **Psalm 63:3-4: "Because your love is better than life, my lips will glorify you."** Worship can also be creative—

writing, journaling, or even dancing as expressions of praise. The Bible encourages us to bring our whole selves into worship, as seen in **Psalm 98:4-6,** where the people of Israel used songs, instruments, and joyful shouts to celebrate God's goodness.

Practical steps made worship feel accessible. Starting the day with a song of worship, creating a personal worship playlist, or simply taking quiet moments to reflect on God's faithfulness were powerful reminders to make worship a daily habit. Community worship was also highlighted as a way to deepen joy and strengthen bonds with others.

This devotion left us inspired to see worship as a heart posture, not just an action. When we integrate worship into our daily lives, we invite God's presence to transform us, filling us with His joy, peace, and awe. Worship becomes a habit that shifts our focus to Him, renewing our spirit from the inside out.

Week 10- Bible Study Review:
The Joy of Serving

This week's devotion reminded us that serving God and others isn't just a duty—it's a source of deep, lasting joy. The Bible teaches us that true greatness comes from taking on the role of a servant, reflecting Jesus' own heart. **Psalm 100:2** reminds us to **"serve the Lord with gladness,"** showing that serving is not about obligation but an opportunity to experience joy and purpose.

The study emphasized how stepping beyond ourselves to help others shifts our perspective, often easing our own struggles as we focus on God's greater plan. **John 15:11** highlights that Jesus wants His joy to be in us and our joy to be complete, and serving others is one way we step into that fullness. Whether it's small acts of kindness or larger commitments, serving reminds us that life isn't just about us—it's about being part of God's work in the world.

Practical steps made the idea of serving accessible. Looking for simple opportunities, using our unique gifts, and serving with family or friends were highlighted as ways to make service a regular part of life. Staying present while serving and reflecting afterward deepens the joy and connection we feel, reminding us of the impact of even the smallest acts of kindness.

This Bible study left us inspired to embrace a life of service, trusting that as we pour out to others, God fills us with His joy and strength. Serving deepens our connection to Him, enriches our lives, and glorifies the One who placed that desire in our hearts. Every act, no matter how small, becomes a way to share His love and experience His unshakable joy.

Week 11- Bible Study Review: Rest and Self-Care—A God-Given Necessity

This week's devotion reminded us that rest and self-care aren't indulgences—they're essential parts of God's design for our lives. In today's busy world, it's easy to overlook rest, but scripture shows us that stepping back to recharge—physically, emotionally, and spiritually—is transformative. **1 Corinthians 6:19-20** calls our bodies temples of the Holy Spirit, emphasizing the importance of caring for ourselves as an act of honoring God.

Rest isn't just about sleep; it's about resetting and finding peace in God's presence. Philippians 4:8 encouraged us to focus on what is true, lovely, and praiseworthy, shifting our minds away from negativity and toward God's goodness. Similarly, **Exodus 23:12** reminded us of the need for regular rest, highlighting that God designed us—and all creation—to pause and refresh.

The devotion offered practical ways to prioritize rest. Setting boundaries, creating relaxing routines, spending time in nature, and practicing mindful prayer were simple yet impactful strategies to incorporate rest into daily life. **Proverbs 3:24** reassures us of the gift of restful sleep when we entrust our worries to God, while **Isaiah 40:31** promises renewed strength for those who wait on Him.

This Bible study left us with a fresh perspective: Rest and self-care are not selfish; they're vital for maintaining unshakable joy and serving others from a place of abundance. When we prioritize rest, we align with God's rhythm, allowing Him to renew and strengthen us for the work He's called us to do.

Week 12- Bible Study Review:
Creative Expression—A Reflection of God's Glory

This week's Bible study highlighted the profound connection between creativity and our relationship with God. Engaging in creative expression—whether through art, music, writing, gardening, or crafting—is not just a hobby; it's a way to connect with the ultimate Creator. **Proverbs 8:30-31** reminds us that God Himself delights in creation, and when we embrace our creative abilities, we reflect His image and experience His joy.

The study emphasized that creativity becomes an act of worship when we invite God into the process. **Colossians 3:23** challenges us to work with all our hearts as if for the Lord, shifting the focus from perfection to devotion. It's not about the final product but about honoring God through the journey. Whether it's writing a song, planting a garden, or sewing a quilt, each act becomes an offering when done with love and intention.

Exodus 35:31-33 and **Psalm 33:3** further encouraged us to see creative skills as gifts from God, uniquely designed to bring Him glory. Sharing our work can also become a ministry, allowing the beauty we create to touch others' hearts and point them to the ultimate source of inspiration—God Himself.

Practical steps like dedicating time for creative pursuits, inviting God into the process, and sharing our work reminded us how accessible this form of worship is. Even small, intentional acts of creativity can deepen our connection to God and fill us with the joy of the Holy Spirit.

This devotion left us inspired to embrace our creative gifts as a means of worship and a way to reflect God's glory in the world. In every brushstroke, stitch, or note, we are reminded of the Creator who crafted us and invites us to join in His divine joy.

Reflection and Discussion Questions:

As you meditated on this week's Bible study review, **what did** the Lord remind you of or reveal anew to you about joy?

_____

_____

Application:

How can we apply what we have studied this week to our lives?

_____

_____

Simple Prayer:

Heavenly Father, we thank you for your unchanging, unstoppable love and care for us, help us to walk in your joy daily as we seek your presence and nearness and share your love with others. In Jesus' name, we pray. Amen.

Chapter Twenty-One

Unquenchable Joy-Week 21

"That person is like a tree planted by streams of water,
which yields its fruit in season and whose leaf does not
wither —whatever they do prospers."
Psalm 1:1-3

Study and Meditation for the Week:
Review of Weeks 13-17

Week 13- Devotion Review:
Daily Practices—Anchors of Joy and Strength

This week's Bible study emphasized the importance of daily practices like prayer, worship, and Bible study as the foundation of a joyful, purpose-filled life. These habits are not just tools to help us achieve our goals but are lifelines that carry us through life's darkest moments. **Psalm 30:11-12** beautifully illustrates God's transformative power: **"You turned my wailing into dancing; you removed my sackcloth and clothed me with joy."** Even in the hardest seasons, staying close to God through these practices brings restoration and unshakable joy.

The Bible study reminded us that joy isn't about ignoring pain but finding hope in God amidst it. **Isaiah 61:3** promises an exchange of **"beauty instead of ashes, the oil of joy instead of mourning,"** showing how God uses even our brokenness to bring about joy and renewal.

Through consistent time with Him, we're reminded of His faithfulness and His ability to work all things for good.

Practical steps like starting small with just five minutes of prayer or scripture reading, creating a worshipful environment, and meditating on scripture made these practices feel attainable. Journaling gratitude, leaning on community, and making prayer an ongoing conversation with God were additional ways to keep Him at the center of daily life.

This Bible study encouraged us to see these habits as more than routines—they are anchors that root us in God's love and power. In every season, whether joyful or challenging, these daily practices sustain us, giving us strength, perspective, and a deep, unquenchable joy that only comes from Him.

Week 14- Bible Study Review: Renewal—A Fresh Start Through Faith

This week's Bible study reminded us of the power of renewal—a fresh start each day, free from the weight of yesterday's failures. Just as the students in a special education classroom were greeted daily with a clean slate, we, too, can embrace each new day with hope and optimism. Renewal allows us to shed negativity, reflect on our growth, and move forward with a purpose-filled heart.

The devotion highlighted how self-renewal is like activating hidden beauty, much like coloring fabric with ink pencils that transform into vivid colors when treated. Similarly, our strengths and hidden talents are revealed when we embrace renewal through faith, letting go of past setbacks, and stepping into the possibilities of today. This process fosters resilience and joy, empowering us to face challenges with optimism and courage.

Scriptural teachings on renewal reinforced this message. Faith offers a transformative journey of forgiveness, personal growth, and strength in adversity. It reminds us that our past does not define us and that God's mercies are new every morning (**Lamentations 3:22-23**). By trusting in His guidance and embracing renewal, we activate the potential within us to live our best days yet.

Practical steps like reflecting on dreams yet to be fulfilled, letting go of negative thoughts, and embracing each day as a fresh opportunity were empowering takeaways. This devotion left us inspired to walk confidently in God's grace, knowing that every day is a chance to grow, heal, and shine brightly with the beauty He has placed within us.

Week 15- Bible Study Review:
Joy and Trust in Every Season

This week's Bible study reminded us that life is a journey of changing seasons, each bringing its unique challenges and blessings. **Ecclesiastes 3:1** anchors this truth: **"There is a time for everything and a season for every activity under the heavens."** Whether in a season of progress or waiting, we can find joy and peace when we trust that God is working through it all.

The Bible study emphasized that waiting can be one of the hardest seasons to endure. **Psalm 27:14** encourages us to **"wait for the Lord; be strong and take heart and wait for the Lord."** Waiting isn't passive but an active posture of trust and hope. **Lamentations 3:22-26** reminded us that God's mercies are new every morning, sustaining us as we wait. During these times, small blessings—like a kind word or a meaningful scripture—become powerful reminders of His presence and faithfulness.

Psalm 40:1-3 beautifully captured the transformation that happens when we trust God through the waiting: He lifts us, restores us, and puts a new song in our hearts. That joy, rooted in His faithfulness, carries us through the hardest moments and fills us with gratitude when we see His plans unfold.

Practical steps like starting the day in prayer, looking for small blessings, meditating on scripture, sharing our journey, and worshiping while we wait helped make trusting God in every season feel attainable.

This Bible study left us encouraged to embrace joy in every season, trusting that God is always at work. Whether we're waiting or rejoicing, His faithfulness remains, guiding us through each step of life's journey.

Week 16- Bible Study Review:
Seasons of Growth—Trusting God's Transforming Work

This week's Bible study drew a beautiful parallel between the rhythm of growth in nature and the seasons of growth in our own lives. Living amidst the orchards and fields of Northern California, the author reflects on how blossoms and harvests are the result of hard work, patience, and care—just like the growth we experience in our spiritual journeys. Growth often involves discomfort and resistance, yet it's in these stretching seasons that God works powerfully to transform us.

James 1:4 encourages us to let perseverance **"finish its work"** so we can become mature and complete. While growth can feel slow or challenging, it's a process of transformation, as described in **2 Corinthians 3:18: "We...are being transformed into his image with ever-increasing glory."** This transformation requires letting go of old habits and embracing the new self God calls us to, as **Ephesians 4:22-24** teaches.

The Bible study emphasized staying rooted in God, drawing nourishment from His Word and presence. **Psalm 1:1-3** beautifully illustrates this: those planted by streams of water bear fruit in season and do not wither. Even in life's sun-scorched seasons, **Isaiah 58:11** promises that God will guide and strengthen us, ensuring we thrive like a well-watered garden.

Practical steps included trusting the process of growth, celebrating small victories, leaning on a supportive community, and staying connected to God through prayer, worship, and scripture.

This Bible study left us inspired to embrace every season of growth with faith and joy, trusting that God is transforming us into His image, equipping us to bear fruit, and preparing us for the good plans He has in store.

Week 17- Bible Study Review:
Seasons of Life—Trusting God's Perfect Timing

This week's Bible study beautifully illustrated how the rhythm of life mirrors the agricultural seasons seen in the fields and orchards of Central California. Each season—whether it's planting, growth, harvest, or rest—has its own work and purpose, teaching us to trust God's timing and lean into His plans. **Hosea 10:12** encourages us to **"sow righteousness"** and **"reap the fruit of unfailing love,"** reminding us that preparation and perseverance are essential for growth and transformation.

The devotion highlighted how planting seasons can feel slow and discouraging when we don't yet see results. But verses like **Jeremiah 5:24** remind us of God's faithfulness to provide the **"autumn and spring rains"** and assure us of the harvest in due time. These moments of waiting are opportunities to trust in His unseen work and draw closer to Him.

Harvest seasons are equally significant. **Deuteronomy 16:15** captures the joy of reaping blessings after hard work, reminding us to celebrate

God's provision with gratitude. Yet, as **Luke 10:2** points out, harvest is also a call to action—to step into God's work, sharing His love and blessings with others.

Practical steps encouraged us to embrace every season with faith and purpose. Recognizing the season we're in, celebrating small wins, staying rooted in God's Word, and trusting the process were powerful reminders to remain patient and hopeful. Letting go of what no longer aligns with God's will and preparing for the opportunities that harvest brings were also key takeaways.

This Bible study left us inspired to walk through life's seasons with trust and joy, knowing that God is in every moment. Whether we're planting, waiting, or harvesting, His faithfulness remains steadfast, guiding us and using each season to shape us for His glory.

Reflection and Discussion Questions:

As you meditated on this week's Bible study review: **What did** the Lord remind you of or reveal anew to you about joy?

_____

_____

Application:

How can we apply what we have studied this week to our lives?

_____

_____

Simple Prayer:

Lord, thank you for your love for us, your never-ending care and protection. Show us that even when we are not thinking of you, you are always thinking of us, desiring fellowship with us, and preparing a home for us with you. Help us to walk in the mindfulness of your love and care. In Jesus' name, we pray. Amen.

Scripture Resources

Week 1: Study and Meditation for the Week: Relationship

1st Peter 1:8
John 15:11
Nehemiah 8:10
Isaiah 59:19
Psalm 19:8

Week 2: Study and Meditation for the Week: Gratitude

Psalm 126:3
1st Thessalonians 5:16-18
Ezra 3:11
1st Chronicles 16:34
Psalm 126:3

Week 3: Study and Meditation for the Week: Faith

1st Peter 1:8
1st Peter 1:8-9
Hebrews 11:1
Psalm 16:11
Jeremiah 29:11
Philippians 1:25

Week 4: Study and Meditation for the Week: Trust

Psalm 28:7
Proverbs 3:5-6
Psalm 28:7
Psalm 52:8

Psalm 62:8

Psalm 91:2

Week 5: Study and Meditation for the Week: Obedience

Psalm 119:111

Psalm 19:8

John 15:10-11

John 15:10-11

James 1:2-3

Week 6: Study and Meditation for the Week: Presence

Psalm 16:11

Psalm 21:6,

Acts 2:28

Job 33:26,

Psalm 89:15-16

Week 7: Study and Meditation for the Week: Community

1 John 1:3-4

Galatians 6:2

Psalm 122:1

Acts 2:46-47

Philippians 2:2

2 Corinthians 13:11

Week 8: Study and Meditation for the Week: Daily Devotion

Psalm 143:8

Psalms 92:1-2

Psalm 43:4

Psalm 143:8

Mark 1:35

Week 9: Study and Meditation for the Week: Worship

Psalm 9:2
Isaiah 55:12
Psalm 63:3-4 Psalm 33:3
Psalm 68:4   Psalm 98:4-6
Psalm 143:8 Psalm 22:3

Week 10: Study and Meditation for the Week: Service

Psalm 100:2
Psalm 35:27
Psalm 34:22
John 15:11
1 Corinthians 15:58

Week 11: Study and Meditation for the Week: Self-Care

Isaiah 40:31
1st Corinthians 6:19-20
Philippians 4:8
Exodus 23:12
Proverbs 3:24
Isaiah 40:31

Week 12: Study and Meditation for the Week: Creative Expression

Proverbs 8:30-31
Colossians 3:23
Psalm 33:3
Exodus 35:31-33
Exodus 35:35

Week 13: Study and Meditation for the Week: In the Midst of Adversity

Colossians 1:10-12
Psalm 30:11-12
Isaiah 61:3
Psalm 63:5-8
Psalm 126:5-6
Romans 5:3-5

Week 14: Study and Meditation for the Week: Strength for the Journey

Psalm 85:6

Week 15: Study and Meditation for the Week: Season of Waiting

Ecclesiastes 3:1
Psalm 27:14
Psalm 33:20-22
Lamentations 3:22-26
Psalm 5:3
Psalm 40:1-3
Isaiah 25:9

Week 16: Study and Meditation for the Week: Season of Growth

James 1:4
2 Corinthians 3:18
Ephesians 4:22-24
Psalm 1:1-3
Isaiah 58:11
2 Corinthians 5:17

Week 17: Study and Meditation for the Week: Season of Harvest

Deuteronomy 16:15
Hosea 10:12
Jeremiah 5:24
Ecclesiastes 3:1-2
Luke 10:2

Week 18: Study and Meditation for the Week: Review Weeks 1-4

* See weeks 1-4

Week 19: Study and Meditation for the Week: Review Weeks 5-8

* See weeks 5-8

Week 20: Study and Meditation for the Week: Review Weeks 9-12

* See weeks 9-12

Week 21: Study and Meditation for the Week: Review Weeks 13-17

* See weeks 13-17

About the Author

 Kimberly Tyler, M.Ed, is an international best-selling author with over 30 years in education and children's ministry leadership. A retired Education Director and dedicated teacher, she possesses a wealth of knowledge and experience in student success through positive learning environments and advocating for inclusive practices. Kimberly is an inspiring author with a profound gift for seeing others succeed despite any challenges that they may face. Residing in Northern California with her husband and extended family, she draws inspiration from the beautiful surroundings and close-knit community. Kimberly's writing reflects her genuine desire to uplift and empower readers as she shares stories that resonate with faith, hope, and resilience. Her unique blend of storytelling and encouragement has positively impacted the hearts of readers worldwide. An accomplished creative, her favorite mediums are fabric arts such as quilting and embroidery.

She can be found on her Facebook page Brokenvesselholylight and at
http://www.brokenvesselholylight.com

LinkedIn:
https://www.linkedin.com/in/kimberly-tyler-a8849539/
Facebook:
https://www.facebook.com/profile.php?id=100094747320115
Instagram:
https://www.instagram.com/kimmijotyler/
Website:
http://www.brokenvesselholylight.com

www.ingramcontent.com/pod-product-compliance
Lightning Source LLC
Chambersburg PA
CBHW071012120626
46546CB00003B/1054